RAND EDUCATION

# Measuring Hard-to-Measure Student Competencies

## A Research and Development Plan

Brian M. Stecher, Laura S. Hamilton



Sponsored by the William and Flora Hewlett Foundation

For more information on this publication, visit www.rand.org/t/rr863

Library of Congress Cataloging-in-Publication Data is available for this publication.

ISBN 978-0-8330-8806-2

Published by the RAND Corporation, Santa Monica, Calif.



*Cover Image: Monkey Business/Fotolia*

# Preface

In 2010, the William and Flora Hewlett Foundation undertook a new strategic initiative focused on students' mastery of core academic content and their development of "deeper learning" skills (e.g., critical thinking, problem-solving, collaboration, communication, and learning how to learn). The foundation has engaged the RAND Corporation to conduct research related to the conceptualization and measurement of skills for deeper learning. The current project builds on earlier work done at RAND and elsewhere to address challenges relating to the development and measurement of these skills and related competencies. It focuses on the challenges of assessing "hard-to-measure" competencies and is designed to focus conversation among philanthropic organizations and policymakers about providing resources to encourage the development of new measures.[1]

Other reports relating to the Hewlett Foundation's interests in deeper learning include the following:

- Kun Yuan and Vi-Nhuan Le, *Measuring Deeper Learning Through Cognitively Demanding Test Items: Results from the Analysis of Six National and International Exams*, Santa Monica, Calif.: RAND Corporation, RR-483-WFHF, 2014

[1] We use the terms *assessment* and *measure* as synonyms to designate a formal effort to judge how much an individual possesses a certain competency using existing records, structured interactions, or observations of behavior. We use the term *test* to designate an on-demand assessment (or measure) of achievement in traditional content areas, such as mathematics or English language arts.

- Jim Soland, Laura S. Hamilton, and Brian M. Stecher, *Measuring 21st Century Competencies: Guidance for Educators*, New York: Asia Society, November 2013
- Kun Yuan and Vi-Nhuan Le, *Estimating the Percentage of Students Who Were Tested on Cognitively Demanding Items Through the State Achievement Tests*, Santa Monica, Calif.: RAND Corporation, WR-967-WFHF, 2012
- Anna Rosefsky Saavedra and V. Darleen Opfer, "Learning 21st-Century Skills Requires 21st-Century Teaching," *Phi Delta Kappan*, Vol. 94, No. 2, October 2012, pp. 8–13.

The research reported here was conducted in RAND Education, a unit of the RAND Corporation, under a grant from the William and Flora Hewlett Foundation.

# Contents

# Summary

Efforts to prepare students for college, careers, and civic engagement have traditionally emphasized academic skills, but a growing body of research suggests that interpersonal and intrapersonal competencies, such as communication and resilience, are important predictors of postsecondary success and citizenship. In this report, we use the term *interpersonal* to refer to competencies that are important for constructive interactions and relationships with other people, and we use *intrapersonal* to refer to attitudes and dispositions that influence how students solve problems and apply themselves in school, work, and other settings. The latter category includes mind-sets, such as academic tenacity, which enables students to focus on long-term goals and to persevere in the face of challenges.

One of the major challenges in designing educational interventions to support these outcomes is a lack of high-quality measures that could help educators, students, parents, and others understand how students perform and monitor their development over time. This report provides guidelines to promote the thoughtful development of practical, high-quality measures of interpersonal and intrapersonal competencies that practitioners and policymakers can use appropriately to improve valued outcomes for students.

## Rationale

Two recent developments have contributing to growing interest in new measures of interpersonal and intrapersonal competencies. First, states have refined or replaced their academic standards, intending to improve students' preparation for college, work, and civic engagement. The Common Core State Standards, which states can choose to use for their own curricula, are the most prominent example, but even states that have not adopted the Common Core have strengthened their standards in many cases. The new generation of standards broadens the kinds of behaviors that are expected of students—for example, placing greater emphasis on written and oral communication about mathematics and other content areas and active collaboration in learning. These reforms have led to a need for new curricula and assessments to facilitate instruction and monitoring of progress toward the new standards.

A second factor that has led to widespread interest in measuring interpersonal and intrapersonal competencies is a set of research findings that indicate strong relationships among academic performance, career success, and certain behaviors and habits of mind. Researchers have begun to identify intrapersonal and intrapersonal competencies that predict adult occupational, educational, and other life outcomes, leading to growing interest in measuring these competencies throughout students' educational careers as a means of giving educators the knowledge and tools needed to foster their development.

## Sources of Expertise

This report was commissioned by the William and Flora Hewlett Foundation as part of its efforts to promote the development of skills for deeper learning, and it draws on the expertise of approximately 75 researchers, policymakers, practitioners, and funders who participated in meetings related to interpersonal and intrapersonal competencies convened by the foundation or in interviews conducted by the researchers. This report reflects our synthesis of ideas that surfaced during the meetings and interviews, as well as our own expertise related to education research and assessment.

## Guidelines for Research and Development

We identified five broad tasks that must be accomplished to develop and implement appropriate measures of interpersonal and intrapersonal competencies. The tasks are presented in a roughly sequential order, though they overlap to some degree and need not necessarily be carried out as separate steps in a research and development effort. Moreover, each task is not the responsibility of a particular group; some combination of assessment developers, researchers, practitioners, and other stakeholders must complete these tasks and address the issues associated with them.

### Defining and Selecting Constructs

An initial step involved identifying the constructs that will be the focus of assessment development and ensuring that they are clearly defined. This effort should begin by reviewing existing research and assessments and developing clear definitions of the constructs that are of interest. Because of the wide range of possible constructs and measures, developers and funders need to set priorities based to some degree on consensus among stakeholders but also on the likelihood that a given construct will lead to improved college, career, and citizenship outcomes and that it can be influenced by educational interventions. In the report, we also delineate practical and logistical concerns that must be considered when setting priorities.

### Identifying the Intended Uses of the Measure

Assessments can serve multiple purposes, including individual diagnosis and remediation, selection into educational programs or other opportunities, monitoring of system performance, and accountability for teachers or schools. The use to which a measure will be put will likely have an effect on its form and content, the manner in which scores are reported, and the quality standards that are appropriate. Developers and users need to determine which potential uses and measurement settings are appropriate, what decisions can reasonably be informed by the measures, and what specific uses are likely to have benefits that outweigh potential harms. For instance, measures used by classroom teachers to inform day-to-day instruction will need to meet somewhat different criteria from those designed to inform decisions about student selection or placement into programs. Given the prevalence of self-report measures of interpersonal and intrapersonal competencies, it is particularly important to identify the purpose of the measure and consider whether the self-report format is suitable for that purpose.

## Developing Measures

After a construct is identified, developers must choose a measurement method; this choice should be driven by an understanding of the construct and how it is manifest in individuals. The options for measurement go well beyond the typical multiple-choice and short-answer formats, including self-report scales that measure agreement with statements, the collection of judgments from teachers or peers, and performance tasks that ask respondents to make or do something. Most competencies could be assessed using more than one method.

Innovative, technology-enhanced formats offer new ways of measuring interpersonal and intrapersonal competencies. Technology can, for instance, enable students to demonstrate interpersonal competencies by interacting with avatars or to show persistence and other competencies by carrying out simulated experiments. Not only do these assessments offer different ways of asking questions or posing problems; they can also produce detailed data that can provide insights not available through a single score. The development of novel measurement approaches should be guided by input from experts in such disciplines as cognitive science and in the construct being assessed, as well as by psychometricians and by the kinds of practitioners who will ultimately use the measures.

## Evaluating the Technical Quality of Measures

Before using a new measure, it is important to assess its technical quality. Attention to the technical quality of measures is crucial throughout the development process and should continue once the measures are implemented. Validity, reliability, and fairness are the primary technical considerations developers and users should examine.

Lack of evidence of high technical quality not only raises concerns about potential harms stemming from use of a measure but can also affect the willingness of educators, other decisionmakers, parents, and others to support the use of measures of interpersonal and intrapersonal competencies in educational settings. It is also important to recognize that evaluation of technical quality should not be considered a one-time event but should be infused into all stages of development and should be periodically reexamined as measures are rolled out, particularly when they are used in new contexts, with different populations, or for different purposes from in the past.

### Documenting Consequences of Assessment Use

Calls for the adoption of measures of interpersonal and intrapersonal competencies are often accompanied by claims that the use of these measures will ultimately benefit students. Users of assessments should be clear about what outcomes they expect and should monitor the consequences of use so that they can take steps to maximize the benefits and minimize harms. There is a lack of existing evidence regarding the consequences of measuring interpersonal and intrapersonal competencies at the K–12 level, so researchers and other stakeholders should consider ways to gather solid evidence of consequences when these assessments are being developed and on an ongoing basis once they are implemented in the field. In addition, educators should receive professional development to become better users of new measures, and the quality of the professional development should be monitored.

## Promoting High-Quality Measures: Recommendations and Challenges

To support the development of new measures, the Hewlett Foundation and other funders will have to answer some questions. Although we do not have definitive answers, we can suggest a general strategy for addressing key questions and, in some cases, offer tentative answers based on expert feedback during the meetings and interviews.

### Which Competencies Should Be Addressed First?

Efforts to address this question should start with an examination of research to understand what measures currently exist across the domains of interest; how good they are from a technical, as well as a practical, perspective; and how difficult it is likely to be to develop new ones. The process of setting priorities among competencies should be guided by two main factors: how adequate the existing measures are for the intended purpose and how difficult it is likely to be to develop new ones. Adequacy is a judgment based on the number of existing measures, their practicality for use by educators, and their technical quality vis-à-vis their intended purposes. Difficulty of development is a judgment based on researchers' depth of understanding of the construct and familiarity with strategies for measuring it. Many of the experts who provided input argued for focusing on competencies that had fewer existing measures and for which development was likely not to be too difficult. Another crucial consideration in setting priorities for development is educational efficacy, by which we mean the extent to which a competency is understood to be malleable and potentially influenced by an educational setting, as well as the extent to which it is relevant and important to educators and others who are concerned about students' futures.

### Which Research and Development Goals Should Receive Priority for the Identified Competencies?

There are four kinds of activities that might be pursued: (1) conduct basic research to understand the nature of the psychological processes or behavioral manifestations that underlie a construct, (2) develop new measures for a construct that is well understood, (3) assess or improve the quality of an existing measure of a construct, or (4) investigate the consequences of using a measure in the school context. Several experts pointed out that there is still a need for basic research in the intrapersonal domain, which would be followed by efforts to address the other three goals. Although the interpersonal domain could also benefit from more basic research, it is our sense that these constructs are better understood than those in the intrapersonal domain, so more of the initial effort could focus on measure development and then proceed to the other goals. In some cases, in which measures exist (for example, "grit"), more attention is needed on questions of quality and, once implemented in schools, on consequences. The eventual goal is a balanced portfolio with some investment in each of these types of research.

### How Long Will the Research and Development Process Take, and How Much Money Needs to Be Committed to Support the Efforts?

To adequately evaluate validity, reliability, and fairness and to understand the consequences associated with operational use of a measure, a long-term and wide-ranging program of research is needed. This type of effort is probably not feasible for every measure but should be prioritized for those measures that are in widespread use or that are likely to be used under high-stakes conditions. One option to consider would be to conduct a competition and let the marketplace dictate the resource demands for a given competency. A literature review and consultation with some commercial test developers could help provide more-realistic estimates for resource demands.

### How Should the Measurement-Development Process Be Managed?

Participating researchers, policymakers, practitioners, and funders emphasized the need for a coordinated research and development effort that would promote collaboration and create momentum. To facilitating such an effort, we suggest the following approach:

- Create a pair of independent research-coordinating boards to guide the measurement-development process, one for interpersonal competencies and the other for intrapersonal competencies. The two boards would be made up of measurement and content experts and stakeholder representatives.
- Each board would create a research and development agenda, receive funding from contributing foundations and agencies, disburse it to developers, monitor the process incrementally, and make midcourse adjustments based on successes. The boards would not be responsible for doing the assessment-development or validation work; this would be contracted to others.

- The boards should have a multiple-year mandate to reflect that fact that the process of development and validation is likely to take multiple years and to help avoid decisionmakers' natural tendency to move on to new initiatives before giving current initiatives a chance to prove their worth.
- Effective implementation of this approach is likely to require the establishment of guidelines for the operation of the boards, the selection of initial competencies, development of priorities for board efforts, commitments for multiple-year funding, and a board composition that includes members from all relevant stakeholder groups and disciplines.

## Challenges

We have offered guidelines and a possible approach that funders and policymakers could adopt to promote the development of high-quality measures that will foster students' development of crucial interpersonal and intrapersonal competencies. Some challenges must be overcome, including reaching consensus among funders on where to focus efforts, maintaining standards for rigor of the measures, generating public support and maintaining policymaker interest in the measures, staying the course when other funding and policy priorities threaten to overtake this effort, and sustaining a collaborative culture among researchers who often face incentives to go it alone. Although individual foundations and government agencies have sponsored sustained programs of research of the type suggested here, there are few examples of collaboration among these organizations to achieve a shared objective, such as the development of measures of interpersonal and intrapersonal competencies. Nevertheless, according to our interactions with researchers, practitioners, policymakers, and funders, the time may be right to launch an ambitious, collaborative effort that will ultimately benefit students throughout their lives.

# Acknowledgments

Although two authors are credited with writing this report, Appendix B lists the dozens of other people who contributed in important ways to its development. Although we promised not to attribute specific comments to individuals, we also pledged to acknowledge how much we benefited from their input. We want to thank all the people who attended the two discussions related to assessing hard-to-measure skills and those who generously gave of their time to talk with us subsequently. We believe we have correctly listed all the names, and we apologize for any omissions. We also want to thank the Hewlett Foundation, which sponsored the meetings and supported our efforts to write this paper. Marc Chun, in particular, helped to frame the larger conversation and focus our investigation. Amanda F. Edelman and Katie Loa of RAND conducted most of the interviews, undertook background research, and stepped in when we needed assistance. We received helpful comments from two independent reviewers, Anna Rosefsky Saavedra of RAND and Thomas Toch of the Carnegie Endowment for the Advancement of Teaching and from internal RAND reviewer Cathleen Stasz. Stacey Gallaway helped to format the draft, and Lisa Bernard edited the final document.

# Abbreviations

| | |
|---|---|
| AERA | American Educational Research Association |
| AIR | American Institutes for Research |
| ATC21S | Assessment and Teaching of 21st Century Skills |
| CPS | collaborative problem-solving |
| DT | divergent thinking |
| ETS | Educational Testing Service |
| Grit-S | Short Grit Scale |
| ISKME | Institute for the Study of Knowledge Management in Education |
| NAEP | National Assessment of Educational Progress |
| NRC | National Research Council |
| NSF | National Science Foundation |
| PD | professional development |
| PERTS | Project for Education Research That Scales |
| PISA | Programme for International Student Assessment |
| STEM | science, technology, engineering, and mathematics |
| TTCT | Torrance Tests of Creative Thinking |

CHAPTER ONE

# Introduction

Educators and researchers have identified interpersonal and intrapersonal competencies that are important to college and career readiness but that schools do not typically measure. Drawing on the framework provided in the recent National Research Council (NRC) synthesis of research on transferable knowledge and skills (Pellegrino and Hilton, 2012), we use the term *interpersonal* to refer to competencies that are important for constructive interactions and relationships with other people, and we use *intrapersonal* to refer to attitudes and dispositions that influence how students solve problems and apply themselves in school, work, and other settings (see also Soland, Hamilton, and Stecher, 2013). The latter category includes mind-sets, such as academic tenacity, which enables students to focus on long-term goals and to persevere in the face of challenges (Dweck, Walton, and Cohen, 2014). In this report, we do not address most of the competencies that fall into the NRC's cognitive category, though we do use creativity in one example.

The evidence suggests that students who demonstrate these competencies are more likely to become successful adults and engaged citizens. Opportunities to develop these competencies, however, are not equitably distributed among students. Some students engage in both in-school and out-of-school activities that foster growth in these areas, whereas others lack or decline to take advantage of one or both of these opportunities. As a result, it is important for all schools to actively foster development of these competencies, particularly those schools serving students who lack access to high-quality out-of-school experiences. To instill these attitudes and behaviors in all students, schools need to incorporate those attitudes and behaviors into curriculum and instruction, and, to do this well, educators need to be able to assess the development of these competencies. Thus, there is a need for measures that teachers can use to monitor student progress toward developing interpersonal and intrapersonal competencies and for measures that policymakers can use to assess schools' progress toward instilling these competencies in their students.

This report explores the research and development process needed to support new measures of interpersonal and intrapersonal competencies. We describe the steps that researchers and assessment developers should take to create quality assessments of competencies that are not currently measured through means that educators can use effectively and efficiently. Our goal is to produce guidelines that promote the *thoughtful* development of *practical, high-quality* measures of interpersonal and intrapersonal competencies and that practitioners and policymakers can use *appropriately* to improve *valued* outcomes for students. Specifically, we mean the following:

- thoughtful development: Development efforts should be conducted in an efficient, organized, and responsible manner.
- practical measures: Measures should be easy to administer and score, convenient to use in a range of learning contexts, and affordable for schools.
- high-quality measures: Measures should have adequate reliability, validity, and fairness to support their specific uses.
- appropriate uses: Uses should have the potential to improve educational outcomes or policies and avoid causing negative consequences.
- valued outcomes: Measures should emphasize skills and competencies that support college, career, and civic readiness, i.e., preparation that qualifies students to engage in postsecondary academic study, to train for high-quality employment, and to become engaged citizens of their communities.

Although these five criteria can be listed separately, in reality, they are interrelated; choices that enhance one may be detrimental to another. For example, assessment quality can often be improved by making assessments longer to represent more content in different ways. However, longer assessments are often impractical—they impose a greater burden on students, as well as on class time, and they cost more to administer and score. Similarly, an assessment that is optimum for diagnosing an individual student's progress in developing a competency may not be optimum for reporting on a school's overall success in promoting that competency—and the two different uses demand different standards of quality. Thus, the research and development process will have to reflect the complex relationships among these factors.

A secondary focus of this report is to explore the steps policymakers and funders might take to encourage researchers and developers to create these measures and to test their utility with practitioners.

It is important to acknowledge that this report focuses only on measurement of students' intrapersonal and interpersonal competencies and does not address the much broader range of topics related to teaching and learning of these competencies. There is clearly a need for theory development and empirical study to better understand how students develop these competencies and how educators can promote them, but that is not within the scope of this report.

The report has four major sections. In Chapter Two, we briefly explain the rationale for the report, including why educators are interested in assessing interpersonal and intrapersonal competencies, what researchers mean by those terms, and how the William and Flora Hewlett Foundation is trying to promote deeper learning of these competencies in schools, including through fostering the development of relevant assessments. Then we briefly describe the process of measure development, comparing achievement tests with measures of intrapersonal competencies. We also share three short vignettes that describe the respective development of assessments of grit, creativity, and collaborative problem-solving to illustrate the variability of the process. In Chapter Three, we describe the research and development process as it applies to measures of interpersonal and intrapersonal competencies. In Chapter Four, we offer some suggestions about how to organize the development of new measures, and we raise some cautions related to policymaking, funding, and other challenges. The overall development effort cannot be left to researchers alone; addressing our recommendations will require the combined efforts of researchers, practitioners, policymakers, and funders.

Although the primary audience for this report is foundations and other organizations that might fund measure development, the content is also relevant to researchers, practitioners, and policymakers. For ease of presentation, we use the general term *developers and users* in the text, but we mean this to refer to all four of the aforementioned groups.

CHAPTER TWO

# Rationale for Developing New Measures

The call for measures of interpersonal and intrapersonal competencies is motivated by two recent developments. First, states nationwide are currently implementing systemic reform of their academic standards, with the intention of raising the overall economic and civic capacity of the next generation of U.S. students. Second, new research documents the relationships between academic performance, subsequent career success, and civic engagement on the one hand, and interpersonal and intrapersonal competencies on the other.

Current systemic reforms of the U.S. education system, designed to better prepare students for college, work, and citizenship, include new standards for student knowledge and skills, curricula aligned to the new standards, and new assessments designed to measure student progress against the standards. These reforms have been prompted by a variety of factors, including concerns about the failure of No Child Left Behind to raise student outcomes appreciably; the continuing relatively poor performance of U.S. students on international assessments, such as the Programme for International Student Assessment (PISA); the potential for accountability systems based on multiple-choice tests to narrow instruction in undesirable ways; and a perceived lack of alignment between old standards and curricula and current economic demands. In reaction, a growing number of educators and policymakers have advocated the establishment of loftier goals for public education by developing curriculum standards intended to produce graduates who are prepared for college, meaningful careers, and citizenship. The voluntary Common Core State Standards are the most prominent example, but even states that have not adopted the Common Core have strengthened their standards in many cases.

The new generation of standards is intended to be more rigorous, calling for higher levels of achievement than were expected under most existing state standards. They are also, in theory, more carefully aligned with the competencies students need to pursue college, careers, and civic engagement. Toward that end, they broaden the kinds of attributes that are expected of students to include both intrapersonal and interpersonal competencies—for example, placing greater emphasis on written and oral communication about mathematics and other content areas and encouraging active collaboration in learning. The new standards will also guide a new generation of assessments that will more fully reflect interpersonal and intrapersonal domains.

The impetus to develop measures of interpersonal and intrapersonal competencies also derives from recent discoveries about the strong relationships between academic performance, career success, and certain behaviors and habits of mind. Researchers have begun to identify intrapersonal and intrapersonal competencies that predict success in school and in work settings (Pellegrino and Hilton, 2012). Informed by this research, some have called for measures of such competencies to be used in the college admission process (Conley, 2014). Intrapersonal and interpersonal competencies can be powerful predictors of adult occupational, educational, and other life outcomes (Heckman, 2008), and scholars have suggested that these competencies account for much of the relationship that has been found between students' course grades and later success (Farrington et al., 2012). Moreover, research finds that some relatively low-cost, easy interventions can positively affect students' embodiment of these competencies, leading to better academic performance (Blackwell, Trzesniewski, and Dweck, 2007; Cohen et al., 2006; Yeager et al., 2013). Thus, measures of interpersonal and intrapersonal competencies can play at least two important roles: provide information about mastery of specific standards and provide information about competencies that have been shown to be relevant to the attainment of standards and valued longer-term outcomes.

In the hands of teachers, both types of information have the potential to greatly improve student performance. However, teachers need to create learning activities that bolster such positive habits of mind, and they need measures that permit them to assess their students' status and help them identify the right activities for the right students.

## Defining Interpersonal and Intrapersonal Competencies

Though the NRC report is comprehensive, developers and users still must overcome the lack of common understanding regarding what is included within each of the domains of interest. We are not going to solve that dilemma in this report, but it is important for the reader to realize that this is one of the initial challenges facing organizations or individuals who want to work in this area. We use the NRC framework as a common point of reference, acknowledging that others in the field may be using different definitions.

Although there is no universal agreement about how to define specific interpersonal or intrapersonal competencies, nor widely adopted measures for many of them, some leading educators have begun to incorporate their measurement into their instructional programs. Many teachers and schools are already assessing such competencies on a more or less formal basis. For example, KIPP schools strive to develop students' character by focusing on seven "highly predictive strengths" (KIPP Schools, undated): zest, grit, self-control, optimism, gratitude, social intelligence, and curiosity. They use a character growth card to track each student's development of these strengths (KIPP Schools, 2014). Similarly, Summit Public Schools has developed a Habits of Success program that identifies the interpersonal and intrapersonal competencies that its schools attempt to develop in students, including self-awareness and self-management skills, social awareness and interpersonal skills, and decisionmaking skills and responsible behavior. It developed a rating guide to help teachers judge students mastery of these competencies.

Many other teachers and schools are interested in these types of competencies but do not have the resources to develop programs or assessments on their own. As we heard from one of the experts we interviewed (see "Stakeholder Interviews" later in this chapter), "Teachers are already reporting these skills on report cards in categories like 'works well with others,' but [they] don't have any training on what constitutes effective collaboration among students."

## Hewlett Initiative to Assess Deeper Learning

This report was commissioned by the William and Flora Hewlett Foundation as part of its larger efforts to promote the development of skills for deeper learning. The foundation's definition of *deeper learning* includes mastery of core academic content, critical thinking and problem-solving, collaboration, effective communication, self-directed learning, and an "academic mindset." The foundation believes that deeper learning is a critical element of an effective education in the 21st century, and it is using its resources in a variety of ways to encourage schools to attend to these skills (William and Flora Hewlett Foundation, undated). Some of its grants are designed to influence state and district leaders to incorporate skills for deeper learning into curriculum and instruction. It is also funding researchers to develop measures of deeper learning using portfolios, projects, and other methods. Other Hewlett grantees are working directly with teachers to help them bring deeper learning into their classrooms. And the foundation is partnering with schools and districts, many in high-poverty communities, to build a network of educators working to identify the tools that are most effective in promoting knowledge and skills for deeper learning and bring them to teachers and students.

To move its measurement agenda forward, the foundation convened two meetings to discuss needs and challenges related to the measurement of competencies in deeper learning. It contracted with authors Stecher and Hamilton to attend the meetings, conduct follow-up interviews with participants, and draft a framework for research and development of such measures. This report reflects our synthesis of ideas that surfaced during the meetings and interviews, as well as our own expertise related to education research and assessment. We briefly describe the three formal activities in the rest of this section.

### White House Meeting

The Hewlett Foundation and the White House Office of Science and Technology Policy, in collaboration with the Institute for the Study of Knowledge Management in Education, convened a group of approximately 40 researchers, policymakers, practitioners, and funders at the White House Conference Center in Washington, D.C., on February 3, 2014. The full-day workshop, which included presentations, discussions, and brainstorming exercises, was designed to foster discussion about what is known about the measurement of hard-to-measure competencies, such as academic mind-sets, collaboration, oral communication, and learning to learn, and to lay the groundwork for the creation of action plans to develop and implement high-quality measures of these competencies. The workshop engaged key stakeholder groups to identify gaps in the research, specific needs that should be addressed in future research and development work, and identify priorities for next steps in this process in the areas of research, policy, and funding. It was also intended to encourage collaboration across institutions and stakeholder groups, with the understanding that collaboration would be critical to promoting high-quality research and development. A summary of the meeting is provided in Appendix A.

### Researcher Meeting

On April 2, 2014, about 20 researchers—most of whom had attended the earlier White House meeting—reconvened in Philadelphia prior to the annual meeting of the American Educational Research Association (AERA). The agenda for this half-day meeting focused on the challenges of developing a research agenda for measuring 21st-century competencies. The group was led through a set of short exercises designed to elicit ideas about identifying the key components of a research agenda, developing definitions of key constructs, promoting instrument development, assessing instrument quality, maximizing the usefulness and practicality of the newly developed measures, monitoring the consequences of using the measures, obtaining necessary development resources, and informing policymakers about new measures. The discussion was designed to elicit different points of view and cover the topics broadly. It is not surprising that the group rarely reached consensus on any course of action. However, the conversations were quite useful because they focused specifically on the necessary research and development activities, and they broadened the authors' thinking about the challenges to be addressed. Notes from the meeting were very helpful in framing the ideas and identifying some of the unresolved concerns that appear in this report.

### Stakeholder Interviews

We also contacted about two dozen of the participants from the earlier meetings to solicit their individual views on developing measures of interpersonal and intrapersonal competencies. We conducted these one-on-one interviews by telephone, asking respondents for their opinions about how funders should support the development of new measures of interpersonal and intrapersonal competencies; what their priorities would be for choosing which constructs to measure; which purposes they would emphasize; and whether they would emphasize developing new measures, improving the quality of existing measures, or examining the way measures are used. The interviews gave respondents the opportunity to express their ideas more fully and gave the authors a chance to probe more deeply into particular issues or questions that arose. A few of the respondents had a chance to review a draft of this report prior to the interview, and their feedback served as an initial review of the perspective presented here.

Frequently in the report, we quote or paraphrase comments from the participants at one of the meetings or from the interviews. We promised people anonymity so they could speak candidly, so the quotes are not attributed to individuals. However, we thought it appropriate to include quotes to ground the report in expert thinking, and we found that the participants expressed many ideas so effectively that it often made sense to use their own words rather than paraphrase.

## Assessment-Development Process

For those unfamiliar with the test-development process, this section provides a simple introduction to test development in the academic disciplines and illustrates the complexity that can arise with efforts to develop measures of interpersonal and intrapersonal competencies.

### Achievement Testing

There are established procedures for developing a test to measure how well a person understands a well-defined domain, such as an academic subject. For example, Educational Testing Service (ETS) describes seven steps to building a test (ETS, undated). The process begins with defining the objectives (e.g., who are the test-takers, what skills and knowledge will be tested, in what ways will they be asked to demonstrate their knowledge, how long will the test be). The next step is to convene item-writing committees that define actual test specifications, review existing items, and write new ones. Experts review all questions for clarity, style, and similar characteristics. Questions are then pilot-tested to ascertain their difficulty, clarity, and accuracy. Problematic questions (e.g., those that are likely to be biased against a group of test-takers or that do not measure the intended construct) are identified based on both statistical analyses and expert judgment and are modified or removed. Test forms are assembled from items that pass the screening processes. Final reviews occur after the tests are administered to make sure items function as anticipated, scoring is correct, and results meet standards for reliability.

When these procedures are followed, they provide a reasonably strong warrant to infer that scores on the test generalize to the domain from which the test was built. That is, even though the test did not contain every bit of knowledge and every skill that makes up the domain (e.g., third-grade mathematics, English-language literacy, art history), it represented the domain well enough that people who do well on the test are likely to do well on other problems drawn from the domain. Test validation is the process of gathering evidence (e.g., from the test blueprint, from expert judges, from performance on other tests) to support the claims a user might want to make about the meaning of the test score. This is not to suggest that the test-development process is always simple and easy to complete—it can be complex, time-consuming, and challenging—but the general approach to developing tests of academic skills and knowledge is fairly well understood.

## Measuring Interpersonal Competencies

Measuring interpersonal competencies (e.g., communication, collaboration) raises some additional challenges. Many of these competencies involve explicit behaviors, and the process of developing an assessment is similar to the process described for achievement testing. First, the domain is clearly described. Then, a subset of behaviors is selected for assessment. The idea of a test item is replaced by a performance situation (e.g., a recorded voice says, "I have lost my car keys. Can you help me?"), and the respondent has to answer appropriately. The performance aspect adds complexity to the administration and scoring of the assessment, but the process is similar to the achievement example in most other respects. On the other hand, those interpersonal competencies that are not obviously observable (e.g., empathy) present new challenges. For these, we direct the reader to the next section on measuring intrapersonal competencies; the situations are quite similar.

## Measuring Intrapersonal Competencies

It can be more challenging to measure how much a person possesses an intrapersonal competency, such as tenacity or self-regulation. The first task is to develop a clear operational definition for the construct. For many of these competencies, educators would agree that "we know it when we see it" but would be unable to define the competency clearly enough that experts would agree. The next challenge in developing a measure is to think of a structured situation in which the competency can be assessed. We might agree that an *optimistic* person is someone "who is more likely to see opportunities than challenges in an unresolved situation." However, if we wanted to measure optimism, it would not be feasible to follow people around until they encountered such situations and ask them what they are thinking.[1] The most common method for measuring competencies like this is to have the person tell us what he or she is thinking, feeling, or would likely do. Developers come up with written statements and the respondent reports his or her own reaction along a scale (e.g., from agree to disagree), or the

---

[1] Google Glass®, Fitbit®, and life-logging software may open a new door to measuring intrapersonal and interpersonal competencies.

respondent marks his or her position along a continuum between two opposed endpoints (e.g., optimists to pessimist). Another approach is to simulate a situation (describing it in words, creating a computer environment, or portraying it with actors) and let the person react.

The next challenge in developing the measure is to make sense of the responses collected. Although it is relatively easy to "add them up" (or use more-sophisticated statistical techniques, such as item response theory), it may not be as easy to interpret the resulting value. Typically, psychometricians try to make sense of new measures by comparing how people perform on a set of other measures chosen carefully to include both similar and dissimilar constructs. This collection of information is part of what is needed to establish the validity of the scores for a particular interpretation, i.e., that this set of responses actually reflects the person's self-awareness, optimism, or tenacity. Although validation is important for every measure (including achievement), it is more challenging in the domains of intrapersonal and interpersonal competencies.

### Examples of Measure Development

The following three brief vignettes summarize steps in the development of two measures of intrapersonal competencies and one measure of an interpersonal competency. They illustrate some of the complexity and unpredictability that may occur when developing measures in these domains. The stories serve as a useful introduction to the research and development agenda presented in the next chapter.

## Measuring Grit

In 2002, a graduate student and her faculty adviser started thinking about the characteristics of successful people. It was well known that intellectual talent (e.g., intelligence quotient, or IQ) was a predictor of success in a wide range of fields, but Martin Seligman and Angela Lee Duckworth were interested in why some people accomplish more than other people with equal intelligence. They interviewed a range of successful people—e.g., investment bankers, painters, journalists, lawyers—and asked them what distinguished the star performers in their fields. All described similar traits, which Duckworth characterized as "perseverance and passion for long-term goals," or "grit." Fast-forward seven years; in 2009, Duckworth and her associate published the Short Grit Scale (Grit-S), an eight-item self-report measure for adolescents and adults. It measured two subscales—consistency of interests and perseverance of effort—that had good reliability and strong evidence of validity for predicting a variety of academic outcomes.

Duckworth herself demonstrated considerable grit to turn the 2002 observations into the 2009 measure. It was not an easy task, and here are a few of the many intermediate steps in the development of this measure:

- Duckworth and her team's early efforts were directed toward creating a performance test. They asked children to perform a repetitive task to see whether their persistence could be used to measure their grit. But Duckworth realized that persistence in an artificial testing situation was not really a manifestation of "perseverance and passion for long-term goals," i.e., the performance task did not align with the construct.
- She thoroughly examined several existing measures of perseverance, passion, tenacity, and other elements of her construct but found them lacking (e.g., not appropriate for both adolescents and adults, not appropriate across a range of life domains).
- She went back to the descriptions of successful people in the interviews and came up with 27 statements that reflected their personalities, which could be rated on a five-point scale from "not at all like me" to "very much like me."
- In a series of six studies, Duckworth and her team pilot-tested the scale with adults, undergraduates, West Point cadets, and participants in the Scripps National Spelling Bee.
- Duckworth and her team performed detailed psychometric analyses, leading to their selection of the 12 items that constituted the original GRIT scale (Grit-O) in 2007.
- Between 2007 and 2009, Duckworth and her team conducted another series of studies to support their development of the eight-item Grit-S.

**Measuring Grit—Continued**

Although the Grit-S is widely available, the exploration and development of measures of grit is far from over. Duckworth and her team are now working on a version that is appropriate for middle-school students. And Duckworth still thinks that the scale can be improved; she recognizes that the two-factor structure makes conceptual sense but also recognizes that one factor has only reverse-scored items and the other has positively scored items.

Moreover, the scale has only been validated for comparing difference between individuals and not for measuring changes within individuals over time. Thus, Duckworth recommends against using it to judge the impact of interventions to improve grit.

Duckworth is thinking about performance tasks to measure grit, using computer technology to put students in a setting in which their attention to various relevant and distracting stimuli may indicate grit-related traits. She is also looking at ways of coding resumes and activity records to directly measure life choices that are manifestations of grit.

SOURCES: Duckworth et al., 2007; Duckworth and Quinn, 2009; Duckworth, 2014.

## Measuring Creativity

The United States prides itself on producing creative thinkers; many Americans see this as one of the strengths of their education system, although the system does not measure the creative output of schools. On the other hand, psychologists and educators have been trying to understand creativity and measure it for decades.

Early efforts to measure creativity focused on the concept of divergent thinking (DT), characterized by such questions as "how many original uses can you think of for a brick?" This approach was developed by J. P. Guilford, whose 1950s and 1960s DT tests scored responses to such questions on four dimensions: originality (statistical rarity of responses), fluency (number of meaningful responses), flexibility (number of different categories in the responses), and elaboration (level of detail in responses). Ellis Paul Torrance was also interested in measuring creativity and was developing his own measures independently of Guilford. His efforts eventually led to the Torrance Tests of Creative Thinking (TTCT), which has become the most popular test for measuring creativity.

The development of the TTCT began in the 1950s, and it has undergone adaptations and modifications, including the following:

- The original DT tasks consisted of five subtests (unusual uses, ask and guess, product improvement, unusual questions, and just suppose) scored on the four dimensions (originality, fluency, flexibility, and elaboration).
- The measure underwent several iterations to try to make it more reliable (so judges could be trained to give similar ratings). For instance, at one point, Torrance tried a scoring procedure based on the U.S. Patent and Trademark Office's criteria of whether an invention was sufficiently inventive to be patented (Torrance, 1959). Although this approach led to adequate predictive validity, it was eventually dropped because scorers had difficulty scoring reliably and the process took too long (Cramond et al., 2005).
- A large validity study was initiated in 1958 with elementary- and high-school students in Minneapolis. In subsequent decades, the researchers obtained information about their creative activities (e.g., aspirations, accomplishments in art, research, innovation) and correlated them to their scores on the creativity tests they took in school. After seven years, high-school students who scored higher on three of the subscales (fluency, flexibility, and originality) had more creative achievements. After 40 years, elementary-school students' initial fluency and originality were good predictors of the level of their creative achievement (Cramond et al., 2005).

**Measuring Creativity—Continued**

- In 1966, Torrance published the first edition of the TTCT (renamed from the Minnesota Tests of Creative Thinking). It was made up of a verbal portion ("Thinking Creatively with Words") and figural portion ("Thinking Creatively with Pictures").
- In 1984, the developers introduced a streamlined scoring system for the verbal portion and added factors to the scoring of the figural test (including resistance to closing, and abstract titles). The resulting measure produces five norm-referenced scores and 13 criterion-referenced scores (Cramond et al., 2005).
- In 2002, a shortened version, the Abbreviated Torrance Test for Adults (ATTA), was marketed as a 15-minute screening instrument (Goff and Torrance, 2002).

In the 1980s, criticism grew about the scoring and predictive validity of the TTCT assessment. Concerns were raised about test length, inadequate statistical procedures, and questionable psychometric quality; there was some concern that TTCT favored DT test performance over other types of creativity. The TTCT was also criticized for its time-intensive scoring requirements.

Conceptually, the debate has persisted about whether DT is a general skill or embedded in particular areas of activity; in other words, DT could be one part, but not necessarily all, of creativity. The past decade has seen an explosion in the number of researchers focusing on creativity assessment who are trying to address concerns raised about the TTCT and other measures. For example, alternative scoring techniques have been suggested, such as summative scoring (totaling the four scoring dimensions), considering highly uncommon scores, using weighted fluency scores, and scoring based on comprehensive versus individual subject answers.

Researchers have also developed different methodologies to administer, score, and interpret DT assessments. Efforts are under way to try to use technology to enable more-efficient scoring on a large scale. There have also been discussions of the appropriate role of general creativity assessments—in particular, whether scores are valid for use in state accountability systems, high-stakes assessment, or classroom use.

There is still disagreement about what creativity is and how it differs from innovation, although creativity scholars generally emphasize the importance of originality or uniqueness in combination with usefulness or appropriateness. For example, Plucker, Beghetto, and Dow (2004) define creativity as "the interaction among aptitude, process and environment by which an individual or group produces a perceptible product that is both novel and useful as defined within a social context," and Simonton (2012) proposes a definition of novelty, utility, and surprise (or nonobviousness).

SOURCES: Plucker, Beghetto, and Dow, 2004; Plucker, 2014.

## Measuring Collaborative Problem-Solving

In 2008, three international technology firms (Cisco, Intel, and Microsoft) that were concerned about high-school graduates lacking the requisite skills for employment in the digital age launched an effort to identify and assess relevant 21st-century skills. They collaborated with six national governments to fund the Assessment and Teaching of 21st Century Skills (ATC21S) project, and leadership of the project was assigned to the University of Melbourne. ATC21S's goal was to develop 21st-century assessment methodologies that would influence educational curricula and outcomes. In 2010, ATC21S project leaders selected three broad skill areas as the focus of their efforts. Collaborative problem-solving (CPS) was one of those areas.

A CPS expert panel was commissioned to write a white paper to establish the theoretical basis for the construct and develop a broader conceptual framework. As the panel defined it, the CPS construct included elements of critical thinking, problem-solving, decisionmaking, and collaboration skills, and it identified five distinct CPS skill strands: three social strands (participation, perspective-taking, and social regulation) and two cognitive strands (task regulation and knowledge-building).

Once the CPS skill set was defined, the project turned to assessment formulation and development. For a variety of practical and theoretical reasons, the decision was made to focus on online assessments, suitable for students ages 11–15, that encompassed both individual and collaborative skills and that would be useful for formative purposes at the classroom level.

Two organizations began to develop assessments consistent with these criteria. The World Class Arena in the United Kingdom undertook the development of CPS tasks related to topics from the mathematics and science curriculum, and the University of Melbourne's Assessment Research Centre was commissioned to develop tasks that measured inductive and deductive reasoning independent of curriculum topics. The team developed strategies for measuring particular CPS skills using online activities, and they created rubrics for differentiating levels of performance. For example, the lowest level of knowledge-building is described as follows: "The student continually attempts the task with the same approach with little evidence of understanding the consequences of actions taken." On the other hand, the highest level is described thusly: "The student has a good understanding of the problem and can reconstruct and/or reorganize the problem in an attempt to find a new solution path." Panels of psychometric specialists and teachers were involved throughout this process to review materials and provide iterative feedback.

Developers faced additional technical challenges because the assessments were going to be delivered online. For example, they had to ensure that data remained secure and that students' identities were protected. They also had to ensure that the computer systems that delivered the assessments were scalable and efficient. It took a couple of years to go from conceptualization to initial assessments.

By 2012, the University of Melbourne team had created 11 digital problem-solving tasks that were presented at the International Testing Commission Conference in Amsterdam. For example, in the olive-oil exercise, two students (A and B) working on computers in different locations have to solve the problem of getting 4 L into a 5-L jug. Student A controls the source of oil and a 3-L jug. Student B controls the 5-L jug and the ability to transfer oil through a pipe. Neither knows what resources the other has or what he or she controls. Nor can either student see his or her partner's screen. They can communicate using only a chat box. The only instruction is to get 4 L into the 5-L jug.

The project team developed scoring algorithms that translated student responses (all keystrokes were logged, so there was an extensive record of the problem-solving interaction) into scores on each of the five strands; students were scored separately and as a team.

Draft CPS tasks were then subject to cognitive laboratories, pilot studies, and calibration trials in multiple countries. All materials were placed in the public domain and accessible via the project website. The cognitive laboratory process focused on how the students engaged with the various tasks; the goal was to ensure that the range of information was covered and to refine the coding protocol. The pilot studies addressed practical questions, such as how easily the assessment could be administered in the classroom, whether the site had the technological infrastructure needed, and how much time was required. After the pilot studies, the tasks were subject to more controlled trials to collect data to establish the empirically based scales and psychometric properties of the tasks themselves, allowing researchers to fine-tune the assessment procedure.

Corporate support ceased after 2012. Since then, further research has continued at the University of Melbourne with a focus on refining the prototypes, controlled research studies, and dissemination. A massive open online course (MOOC) was delivered in August 2014 (and again in April 2015) as a means of dissemination. Current efforts focus on ways of incorporating CPS tasks into PISA in 2015.

SOURCES: Griffin and Care, 2015; Griffin, 2014.

CHAPTER THREE

# Research and Development Guidelines

Five broad tasks must be accomplished to develop and implement appropriate measures of interpersonal and intrapersonal competencies. If we are to produce high-quality measures that can be used in ways that are beneficial for students, some combination of assessment developers, researchers, practitioners, and other stakeholders must complete these tasks and address the issues associated with them. The five tasks are *defining and selecting constructs*, *identifying intended uses of the measures*, *developing the measures*, *evaluating their technical quality*, and *documenting the consequences of their use*. This chapter describes guidelines for research and development in each area. We present the tasks in the order in which they will typically be addressed during the research and development process, but we do not mean to imply that they are separate steps that need to be carried out in a precise sequence. They are likely to overlap to some degree, and many aspects can be carried out simultaneously.

## Defining and Selecting Constructs

The vignettes presented at the end of Chapter Two illustrate some of the variety of strategies that have been used to develop assessments of interpersonal and intrapersonal competencies. In all three examples, the developers had to decide on the construct they were interested in measuring and had to develop a clear operational definition for it. To be successful, any research agenda needs to identify constructs for assessment development and make sure they are clearly defined.

The task of defining and selecting constructs involves both measurement considerations (e.g., what constitutes an adequate construct definition, how narrow or broad the identified constructs should be) and procedural considerations (e.g., the order in which activities should occur, the selection of researchers to work on particular constructs). In this section, we describe a few of these considerations. The list is not exhaustive, but it should give the reader an idea of some of the major issues that will have to be addressed to define and select specific constructs for assessment development.

### Existing Research and Assessments Should Be Reviewed

An appropriate first step in measure development is to review relevant research and related assessments. This may seem like an odd starting point, given the premise of the paper that there are no adequate measures for many interpersonal and intrapersonal competencies. However, the lack of a thoughtful, practical, high-quality measure in a particular domain does not mean that developers are working in a vacuum. The mere fact that we can identify a competency, however imprecise that identification might be, means that some level of conceptualization has occurred. More than likely, there is relevant research literature from one or more disciplines—psychology, education, sociology, or economics—that will help to bound the construct of interest. There are also likely to be measures in existence that will prove useful in thinking about assessment-development options. Developers can gain insights into assessment approaches from considering measures of related constructs. It is useful to have access to measures of similar but not identical constructs to use in the validation process. Scanning the research and assessment literature is a good starting point in any assessment-development effort.

### Each Construct Needs to Be Clearly Defined to Support Measure Development

Most test development begins with efforts to clearly describe the domain to be measured, and that approach seems logical in the context of interpersonal and intrapersonal competencies as well. However, it may be easier to delineate the target competencies in a content area, such as English-language arts (e.g., using appropriate verb form for a given subject), mathematics (finding the lowest common denominator), or science (understanding the water cycle), than it is when describing psychological constructs (e.g., perseverance, self-regulation, creativity). Unlike the academic content areas, psychological competencies may not manifest themselves in an on-demand testing session. It may not be possible to judge whether a person has grit or determination on the basis of a specific response to a specific prompt.

In the case of interpersonal and intrapersonal skills, the construct definition is likely to be of a different character from that of academic constructs. For example, Franken (1993, p. 396) defines creativity as "the tendency to generate or recognize ideas, alternatives, or possibilities that may be useful in solving problems, communicating with others, and entertaining ourselves and others."[1] A few features of this definition are noteworthy. It describes the competency in terms of a tendency to behave in a particular manner, not in terms of a specific behavior in a given setting (such as "using appropriate verb form"). Another interesting feature is its multidimensionality; the presence of connectives, such as "or" and "and," indicates that there are different ways the construct might be manifest. Both of these features may make it more difficult to develop a measure of creativity. In fact, although ideas about creativity are converging, different definitions have held sway at different times. As assessments have been developed and tried, evidence has influenced common beliefs about creativity, and the definition has evolved.

There is no agreed best way to achieve clarity of definition, but researchers have developed techniques for clarifying competency constructs. For example, there is considerable literature in industrial and organizational psychology on competency modeling that is relevant to this task (Stevens, 2013).

---

[1] An alternative definition from Plucker was presented in the earlier vignette.

Some participants in the Hewlett-sponsored meetings suggested that it is important to have diverse teams involved in the process. One educational researcher said,

> This is a nascent field. So I see the advantages of a broad number of people looking at constructs from different methodology and disciplinary vantage points. A multitude of approaches is good, so narrowing down and picking one person is not good.

Another noted the advantages of collaborative work: "I would be focused on how can you bring people together to come up with something that has a common lexicon, and a majority of people can get behind, and is credible, so that we can move this forward." A participant also reminded us, "it makes sense to start by developing a cognitive model of student thinking and use it as the basis for designing measures (e.g., evidence-centered design) rather than trying to develop construct definitions in a vacuum."

### For Any Given Interpersonal or Intrapersonal Competency, There Are Likely to Be Related, Possibly Overlapping, Constructs, and a Focal Construct Must Be Identified

For example, as Franken (1993, p. 394) notes about creativity,

> The ability to generate alternatives or to see things uniquely does not occur by chance; it is linked to other, more fundamental qualities of thinking, such as flexibility, tolerance of ambiguity or unpredictability, and the enjoyment of things heretofore unknown.

One of the meeting participants described other examples:

> On both the intrapersonal and interpersonal sides, there are groups of competencies that are related but not identical. An issue that should be explored [is] where there are overlaps, what are the distinctive features of each, and how do the competencies relate to one another. In the intrapersonal arena, this might include persistence, grit, self-regulation, metacognition, and conscientiousness. On the interpersonal side, this might include the ability to

collaborate and how general or specific is that and how does it relate to teamwork, communication, and leadership.

A related concern is that competencies that are distinguishable may be highly correlated. As a participant noted,

> The competencies are so co-varying; I don't want to lose that. For example, building the capacity to work as a team is connected with building the capacity for problem-solving and decisionmaking; it is co-varying in positive ways. For example, self-reflection and intrapersonal competencies are important for executive function, which is very important.

Developers and users may have to consider a set of competencies and either choose among them or look for a broader unifying construct. Although one participant cautioned, "the more generic the measures become, the less useful they become." Thus, the development process has to clarify the relationships among related constructs and then decide where to set priorities for measure development. Again, there are techniques that can be used to clarify fine distinctions among constructs, including efforts to develop explicit, detailed definitions of related constructs and to identify similarities and differences among them as a means of informing revised definitions that are clear and discrete.

### Selection of Constructs for Measure Development Should Be Based on Consensus Among Key Stakeholders

Experts who participated at the White House meeting had different interests and would likely have ranked potential assessment-development efforts differently. Somehow, these diverse perspectives will have to be reconciled. Researchers may have the best ideas about the current state of theoretical knowledge and the potential for generating new assessments. Funders of assessment-development efforts will certainly want their priorities to be incorporated into any plans. The assessments are not likely to have positive effects if policy does not permit or encourage their use, so the opinions of policymakers are highly relevant. Practitioners, as well, have important insights into how potential assessments will operate to support assessment and learning. Developers and users will have to bring many voices into deliberations before setting priorities among competing constructs. The plethora of perspectives highlights the need for some form of dialogue or consensus-building. As one participant suggested,

> The different people and groups interested in this topic all have different mental models about these competencies. There needs to be a bringing together of everyone working on this to hash out what the thing is that we are trying to achieve and therefore how we'll know if the tool is successful in getting us there or not.

### Competencies Do Not Always Apply Generally; They May Be Specific to a Particular Setting or Context

Each construct can be defined as a general competency that occurs in a variety of contexts or as a subject- or setting-specific competency. For example, a person may be an excellent quantitative problem-solver but be much less adept at solving interpersonal problems. As one participant noted, "Collaboration on mathematical understanding looks different [from] collaboration on analysis of a literary text. So funders need to determine what domain they are interested in: STEM [science, technology, engineering, and mathematics], math, workplace skills? At what level should 'problem-solving' be defined?" Similarly, as one participant noted,

> Grit is difficult to talk about in the abstract, without specific situations. So I would look at the specific conditions before creating a big construct. If we want to make statements about grit, we have to qualify it; we can't talk about it without context. It's not who has the most grit, but how each individual's grit manifests in reaction to background, knowledge, encouragement, etc. A child could have grit when playing soccer but not for studying. It would be a mistake to assign that kid an overall level of grit.

On the other hand, much of the attention that educators are giving to intrapersonal competencies, such as grit, derives from the correlation between simple measures and later outcomes. For example, the ability to delay gratification measured in young children has been found to correlate with positive outcomes later in life (Shoda, Mischel, and Peake, 1990). More research is needed to understand whether a given competency is more general or context-specific.

Another participant noted that context might also shape development of the competency: "There is a real importance in understanding . . . the constructs themselves and measuring them, but equally important is to understand the contextual factors that shape their development." Developers and users will have to examine evidence about a construct to see whether it makes sense to define it broadly or narrowly and will need to evaluate the generalizability of scores on a measure of that construct across different contexts. Practitioners will have to think about the context in which competencies are developed.

### Priority Should Be Given to Constructs That Lead to Improved College, Career, and Citizenship Outcomes

If choices are to be made for targeting limited resources, there will need to be criteria for judging among constructs. One such criterion is whether there is evidence that a competency predicts a desired outcome, such as graduation, college enrollment, or long-term employment. Some employers use skill-based hiring, in which they hire not on the basis of graduation or a degree but a candidate's performance on competency assessments (Kyllonen, 2013). One respondent was enthusiastic about the potential for measures of job-related competencies to improve the access of disconnected youth to the job market:

> If we could get more employers hiring on the basis of these competencies, as opposed to whether or not you have a bachelor's, this could be really important for a percentage of the population that is unlikely to get a four-year degree and is disconnected from both education and the labor market.

Where empirical evidence is lacking, developers should also look for theoretical justification.

### Priority Should Be Given to Constructs That Are Likely to Have Educational Efficacy

By *educational efficacy*, we mean two things. First, it is important to consider whether the construct is likely to be malleable in the school setting, i.e., whether teachers can positively influence student development of the construct. One participant expressed this idea succinctly: "I think the idea of teachable, changeable, malleable, are probably the most important because you want to be measuring competencies that can be developed." As another noted,

> You need to begin with what competencies are particularly valuable in people's lives and which ones are amenable to be influenced by education. For example, the character of parenting received by a child is influential in how successful that child will be in school and life. But we have no credible ways to change parenting. So putting resources into this might not be a good idea.

*Educational efficacy* also refers to relevance and credence to educators. One participant pointed out the need to attend to the perspectives of educators, as well as parents:

> I think there should be some common understanding of informal measures that people use in daily life and how they can be understood and used. What do teachers [and] parents use? What do they think about? I think work in that area could be very informative.

This comment suggests a need to collect information on the interests and priorities of different stakeholder groups, particularly the teachers who will ultimately be responsible for promoting improved student performance on the selected measures.

### Practical and Logistical Concerns Should Be Considered When Setting Priorities Among Constructs

For a variety of reasons, it is likely to be difficult to decide which competencies to tackle first. For example, participants in the meetings disagreed about whether the process should start with easy wins or tackle the more-difficult challenges. Some participants at the pre-AERA workshop suggested starting with low-hanging fruit, i.e., competencies that can be observed directly, such as oral communication and collaboration, and defer until later harder-to-observe constructs, such as academic habits of mind and learning to learn.

A participant suggested the idea of focusing on more-manageable pieces:

> One thing that is useful in the short term [is] specific skills. People want to tackle big issues, like grit, emotional intelligence, perseverance, problem-solving, and leadership. These are broad labels. But within these things, there are specific skills that are more context-dependent. It might be worth spending more time on this level and understand how these things are taught [and] developed and how they manifest in different situations. It will give us a better handle, both on the components and [on] situation specificity.

Other participants preferred starting with the more-challenging competencies.

> If we want to make progress on things we don't know how to measure well, then we need to focus more on intrapersonal and metacognitive skills. That should be the first priority. Perhaps a mixed portfolio is best; if there are adequate resources, then some should be invested in low-risk efforts that are designed to yield practical assessments quickly while others are targeted to higher-risk efforts that focus on competencies judged to be more difficult to assess.

Other practical questions, not addressed at the meetings, might affect the priority given to different competencies. Is there reason to believe that one construct will be easier to assess than another? How long is it likely to take to complete the development and validation process? Is relevant expertise available to tackle development in a timely manner? How great is the cost of development of one competency compared with that of other competencies? For example, some participants thought that it would be faster and less expensive to develop measures that rely on self-report than measures that require external judgments about specific behaviors. We know of no simple model to estimate the required investment of time and money needed for a given measure, but this information is likely to be important in selecting constructs to pursue.

A related question is who should set priorities among constructs, e.g., whether priorities are determined centrally or whether they are guided by the interests and initiative of individual developers. Historically, measures of interpersonal and intrapersonal competencies were developed based on the interests and experiences of individual scholars and their research teams, i.e., development was a bottom-up activity. In this spirit, one approach that current funders could take would be to try to stimulate and support investigator-initiated development. However, participants did not all favor this approach, as one noted: "I wouldn't do it as just field-initiated work because you're going to get a lot of good work, but it won't necessarily cohere. Someone will still need to be responsible for putting it all together." The alternative is a top-down approach that delineates the constructs to be measured and sets priorities among them. Then a competition could be held to identify researchers to design and test assessments related to those competencies. The Institute of Education Sciences follows this model when it establishes competitions for specific research programs.

## Identifying the Intended Uses of the Measure

Assessments can serve multiple purposes within the educational sphere, including individual diagnosis and remediation, placement into programs, monitoring of system performance, and accountability for teachers or schools. The use to which a measure will be put will likely have an effect on its form and content, the manner in which scores are reported, and the quality standards that are appropriate. Thus, some agreement about the desired uses of the assessment is an essential element of the development process.

### Developers Have to Decide Among Potential Uses, and This Decision Should Be Informed by an Evaluation of the Appropriateness and Potential Consequences of Those Uses

There are many potential uses for measures of interpersonal and intrapersonal competencies; one interviewee described several that vary in the level of stakes attached:

> We can divide up the use of new assessments into workforce uses and school uses (K–12 and higher education). High-stakes uses would be for selection, promotion, competition, admission, and scholarships. Low stakes would be for training in the workforce, formative assessment, school monitoring, [and so on].

A large majority of meeting participants and interviewees suggested that these measures should not be used for high-stakes purposes. Of course, perceptions regarding whether a particular use is high stakes can vary; some educators might view school-level reporting of assessment scores, for instance, as high stakes even if no explicit consequences are attached to performance. And measures that are used to place individual students in programs may not have stakes for teachers but certainly would for students.

Developers and users need to determine which potential uses and measurement settings are appropriate, what decisions can reasonably be informed by the measures, and what specific uses are likely to have benefits that outweigh potential harms. This information needs to be taken into account when developing the measure. For instance, a measure that is intended to provide information about an individual's performance has different requirements and features from one that is used to gauge group-level performance. Measures used by classroom teachers to inform day-to-day instruction will need to meet somewhat different criteria from those designed to inform decisions about student selection or placement into programs.

Although there is often an understandable desire to use a single measure for multiple purposes, partly as a way of reducing the financial and time burdens associated with assessment, it is critical that measures not be used for purposes for which they were not intended and for which there is inadequate validity evidence. Similarly, the fact that information on students' collaboration or communication skills was collected does not mean that this information should be used for purposes for which it was not originally intended. Researchers can play an important role in exploring whether expansion of an existing measure to a new purpose or setting is warranted. Given the growing interest in using these measures to inform college admissions and other high-stakes decisions, there is a clear need for research to examine these proposed uses so that policymakers and practitioners can make informed judgments.

### Initial Development Efforts Should Focus on a Single, Clearly Defined Purpose

When a new measure is being developed, it is important that the developers have a clear purpose in mind so that the activities that take place in each phase of development are driven by this intended purpose. It might be tempting to be ambitious at the outset by considering a wide variety of potential uses and target audiences. However, such lack of clarity and breadth of scope can make it difficult to make decisions about length of the measure, item format, scoring strategies, and other features of the assessment that need to be addressed during the development phase. Developers should start with a single purpose and then, once the measure has proven adequate for that purpose, engage in research to explore whether it can be used for other purposes.

One reason to focus on a single purpose in the early development stage is to enable the developers to think broadly about what might be possible. Innovative assessment strategies, such as technology-based games that produce rich data, might be well suited to certain classroom environments. But if developers are concerned about ensuring that an assessment can also be used for other purposes, such as accountability, they might be less willing to explore more-innovative strategies.

### Self-Report Measures Might Be Most Suitable for Research and Theory Development and Should Generally Not Be Used for High-Stakes Purposes

Given the frequent use of self-report measures of interpersonal and intrapersonal competencies, consideration of which purposes lend themselves to self-report measures is particularly important. Yeager et al. (2013) distinguish between measures that can inform theory development and those that are intended to serve practical purposes, such as informing decisions about remediation. The former, which is where researchers usually start, often include self-ratings completed by students, while the latter, which should be the goal for practical assessments to be used in schools, will generally need to capture more-direct evidence of specific behaviors.

One problem with self-reports is that the person whose competency is being measured can easily manipulate them. Several interviewees expressed concerns about this aspect of self-reporting and concluded that such measures should probably not be used under high-stakes conditions. One noted, "Self-reported measures are more likely to be gamed, and high-stakes encourages gaming." This interviewee also suggested that low-stakes uses should be emphasized because of the problem of gaming in general: "Researchers should focus on low stakes, because those are less likely to be gamed and more likely to be used for improvement."

Another drawback associated with self-report measures is that they often involve relative judgments, which can be biased based on the local comparison group. When a student indicates the extent to which he or she agrees or disagrees that "I try hard in school," that student is probably implicitly comparing him- or herself with the other students in the peer group or to some internal standard he or she has set for him- or herself. Both of these comparison sets can be changed, making the measure inconsistent. Yeager et al. (2013) report on an unpublished example from Duckworth, in which self-reported levels of grit—passion or perseverance for long-term goals—declined among West Point students over four years, a seemingly unlikely result, given that these students are succeeding at physical and mental challenges. Their explanation is that students' judgments lessen not because they are showing less grit but because they are comparing themselves with increasingly gritty peers and role models. As the comparison set changes, the judgments are modified. In contrast, a behavioral measure of grit, perhaps one that included time spent on mental or physical efforts, would not have shown this paradoxical change.

## Developing Measures

After a construct is identified, there are ways one might go about trying to develop a measure. We briefly touch on some of the considerations that will guide developers and users.

### The Choice of a Measurement Method Should Be Driven by an Understanding of the Construct and How It Is Manifest in Individuals

Most people are familiar with multiple-choice, true/false, and short-answer questions that appear frequently in standardized tests, but the assessment developer's bag of tricks contains many other ways to collect information that can be used to make a judgment about an individual's standing with respect to a particular competency. For example, many psychological measures use self-report to obtain information about beliefs, preferences, or attitudes by asking people to describe themselves in terms of a scale with opposing end values (e.g., How strongly do you agree or disagree with a given statement? Where would you place yourself on a scale between extroverted and introverted?). Another way to assess competency is to ask for judgments from teachers, peers, counselors, or other individuals who have direct experience with a person for an extended period of time. It is also possible to use performance tasks that ask respondents to make or do something. People trained to identify certain features can then rate the product. Thus, there are a variety of ways to collect information that could become an assessment of an interpersonal or intrapersonal competency. Most competencies could be assessed using more than one method.

Where feasible, the assessment method should be as much like the competency as possible rather than a distant correlate. For example, it is possible to measure oral communication using a multiple-choice test, with questions that ask the respondent to pick the best choice of responses to a given prompt. Performance on such a test is likely to be positively related to oral communication because those who cannot select the right response on paper are unlikely to be able to create it in person. However, it would be more authentic to measure oral communication by asking the respondent to engage in a conversation. This approach also signals to teachers and students that engaging in oral communication is valued directly above some surrogate activity.

One expert noted additional advantages of performance assessments: "We also need to look beyond the assessment into the range of what is happening during the process of preparing for [or] completing a performance-based assessment, including things like peer collaboration and working with a mentor." Another discussed this issue in the context of the SAT exam:

> One weakness with inter- [and] intrapersonal skills assessment is that we often use a rating scale, either through self-assessment or by people who know them. And rating skills have well-documented limitations, with biases and reference-group effects. We know [that] ratings are only weakly correlated to cognitive test scores. So we know we are [getting only] a weak signal. So the cognitive analogy would be, instead of taking the SAT, we'd ask the student to rate [his or her] verbal competency. So where we are now is asking the student to rate his or her own inter- [or] intrapersonal skills versus being assessed. A productive research program would try to find ways to measure these fields through performance tasks. Instead of ratings, put people in [situations in which] they have to rely on skills.

Of course, there are other factors to be considered—e.g., cost, consistency, bias—that might argue for a different approach.

### Innovative, Technology-Enhanced Formats Offer New Ways of Measuring Interpersonal and Intrapersonal Competencies, but Development of Such Measures Should Be Guided by Experts and by Practical and Measurement Demands

Developers have been taking advantage of the growing availability of information technology resources in schools and other settings by creating new types of assessments that measure complex competencies in ways that are difficult or impossible with paper-and-pencil assessments. Technology can, for instance, enable students to demonstrate interpersonal competencies by interacting with avatars or to demonstrate persistence and other competencies by carrying out simulated experiments (see Soland, Hamilton, and Stecher, 2013, for detailed examples). As we note in the next section, technology-based assessments not only offer different ways of asking questions or posing problems but can also produce detailed data that can provide insights not available through a single score. In addition, technology can facilitate the use of accommodations for students with special needs, such as by enabling test administrators to increase the type size or read text aloud.

However, some of our interviewees cautioned that technology-based assessments deserve careful scrutiny by experts in some disciplines, such as cognitive science. One mentioned specific questions that should be asked: "How do you monitor the mechanism? Is there innovation in the way that it is being done? What kind of capacity does it require? Are there different capacities that are underexploited?" Moreover, decisions regarding technology applications should be informed by considerations regarding what types of hardware and software are likely to be available in the administration site, whether it is a school, students' homes, or some other venue, as well as by an understanding of what technology-related skills students will need so that the technology does not get in the way of students' ability to demonstrate their competency. As we discuss later, traditional approaches to assessing validity, reliability, and fairness might also need to be modified to address these more-complex formats.

### Existing Data Could Be Mined to Measure Some Intrapersonal Competencies

Educational data systems that track attendance, course-taking, behavior, grades, and other measures are another source of data that can be used as the basis for measuring some competencies. For example, some schools now look at patterns of course-taking among middle-school students to identify those who are at risk of not graduating. Such archival data can also be used to capture competencies, such as persistence or educational aspirations. Robertson-Kraft and Duckworth (2014) created a measure of grit based on college students' participation in extracurricular and work activities in a study that examined the relationship between grit and teachers' effectiveness, assigning extra points for accomplishments, such as receiving awards or serving in leadership positions.

Achievement testing, particularly if it includes complex, open-ended problems, can create a hidden source of data that can be used as the basis for new measures. Computerized achievement testing creates a detailed record of each student's engagement with the questions that might reveal other behavioral characteristics. As one participant noted, many existing complex assessments produce extensive data beyond just the final scores, such as information on how many attempts a student makes or where he or she moves the mouse. The process of converting this type of data into a meaningful measure of a specific construct is generally not straightforward and should be a focus of research among measurement experts and cognitive scientists.

### Assessment-Development Teams Should Include People with Expertise in Assessment and People with Expertise in the Construct Being Assessed

Commercial test publishers often assemble a team of content experts and psychometricians to work together to create a new assessment. That model should be followed when developing assessments of interpersonal and intrapersonal competencies. Researchers with understanding of the competency are essential to keep the focus on the desired target; experienced developers understand both the science and the art of assessment design to bear on the challenging construct. As one participant described it,

> My hunch is that a good way to encourage development of these high-quality measures is to encourage the formation of teams to bring together expertise. The measures experts are very good at measuring specific domains (mathematical thinking or discourse in classrooms), but typically it is hard to find people [who] have conceptual knowledge and highly technical measurement knowledge when it comes to measures with utility and scalability.

Another participant went further and noted the potential advantage of multidisciplinary teams:

> People often complain about this Tower of Babel and the different labels. Each little subdiscipline has its own traditions, its own language, its own codes, which is part of the problem. I think [that] it would be beneficial to fund cross-disciplinary work on measurement development, which could help [resolve] this.

### Practitioners Should Also Be Part of the Measurement-Development Process

If the goal of the development is to produce a measure that is useful to educators, then it is important to have practitioners in the process from the outset. They bring insight into the practical aspects of assessment in the educational context. As a participant noted, teachers

> bridge the gap between what psychologists are doing in the lab [and] artificial simulation and what actual classroom instruction at scale [looks] like. We noticed that there is a distance between what the psychologist types are thinking about and trying to measure and what everyday life conceptions are. This is important: We need two-way communication. Researchers need to hear what citizens and teachers think things are.

Although practitioners' considerations may not dominate development, particularly during the early, more-experimental phases, developers need to be cognizant of their perspective so their efforts eventually meet the needs and demands of educators in terms of logistics, practicality, and other characteristics. Another advantage of involving practitioners is creating important links to school communities. One participant noted,

> It's going to take some significant investment in resources and assistance identifying collaborating school sites and other types of sites where the development and validation work can go on. One of the dilemmas for researchers is gaining access to sufficient-sized populations and samples to be able to do proper cycles of

> development and validation of instruments. This is a key factor that influences the likelihood of the researcher being successful to advance the field in terms of having valid, reliable measures.

Depending on the purpose of the assessment, it may also be important to include representatives of employers on the development team:

> One of the biggest problems for most of these competencies is who participates in the discussions. Often the intended audience is the industry, and [industry representatives] are almost never at the table for these discussions. Without industry people as part of the discussion, the definition of needs is often a world away from what industry actually wants. If the objective is to prepare students to be workers, members from industry who are on the ground level, doing the hiring, need to be at the table.

### Developers and Funders Should Not Impose a Rigid Template on Development Efforts Because All Measurement Development Does Not Proceed in the Same Manner

The ETS approach described earlier is the result of many years of designing tests of a particular type for a particular audience. It does not necessarily apply in every situation. The three vignettes illustrate different approaches to assessment development. Although it is useful to have a general framework in mind for the purpose of monitoring development efforts, it would be a mistake to impose a fixed set of steps or stages on all developers.

## Evaluating the Technical Quality of Measures

Before using a new measure, it is important to assess its technical quality. Attention to the technical quality of measures is crucial throughout the development process and should continue once the measures are implemented. We focus on three aspects of technical quality here: validity, reliability, and fairness. Developers and users should refer to the *Standards for Educational and Psychological Testing* (AERA, American Psychological Association, and National Council on Measurement in Education, 2014) for guidance regarding these features of technical quality.

Lack of evidence of high technical quality not only raises concerns about potential harms stemming from use of a measure but can also affect the willingness of educators, other decisionmakers, parents, and others to support the use of measures of interpersonal and intrapersonal competencies in educational settings. As one interviewee noted,

> There is a perceived lack of quality for existing interpersonal and intrapersonal measures. Even top-notch researchers make silly mistakes when it comes to noncognitive skills assessment. Noncognitive constructs and measures are not treated with the same care as cognitive measures; more attention needs to be paid to the quality of these measures.

Priority should be given to research on the technical quality of existing measures and of those in development. It is also important to recognize that evaluation of technical quality should not be considered a one-time event but should be infused into all stages of development and should be periodically reexamined as measures are rolled out, particularly when they are used in new contexts, with different populations, or for different purposes than in the past.

### A Comprehensive Validity Investigation Should Be Undertaken for Any New Measure, but Developers Might Not Be Able to Gather All Appropriate Evidence During the Initial Development Phase

Validity, which is the extent to which there is evidence to support specific interpretations of assessment scores for specific purposes, is the most important technical consideration. Although it is not possible to prove definitively that a measure supports valid inferences, developers and users need to gather as much evidence as possible to support the claims that they plan to make based on assessment results. It is not uncommon for developers to argue that their measure is valid because it correlates with a desired outcome or because experts have reviewed the content, but, in fact, a claim regarding validity generally needs to incorporate multiple sources of evidence. A validity claim also must be made in reference to a specific purpose: A measure that supports valid inferences about students for making instructional decisions in the classroom, for example, does not necessarily do so for a higher-stakes purpose, such as college admissions.

The sources of evidence that should be brought to bear on a validity investigation might include relationships with other information collected concurrently with assessment scores, prediction of future performance (e.g., in college), information about the cognitive processes in which students engage when completing the measure, and expert ratings of assessment content (AERA, American Psychological Association, and National Council on Measurement in Education, 2014). Some of this information can be obtained relatively inexpensively and at an early stage in the development process, whereas other sources require data collected through field tests and long-term analyses of subsequent performance. Developers and users should clearly identify the purpose of a measure along with the inferences that it is intended to support; develop an argument linking these inferences to the types of evidence that support them (Kane, 2006); and devise a plan for gathering this evidence. As one interviewee noted,

> If you're looking at formative assessment, it is really important to develop criteria associated with the ability [and] alignment of the test with teaching and learning goals in the classroom. We have not done a good job of that at any level.

The evidence does not all need to be collected at once, but, over time, the process of validating the measure for a specific use should include efforts to collect and apply new evidence as it becomes available. Researchers should collaborate with assessment developers and with those who use the assessments in the field to design validity investigations that incorporate the highest-quality data and analyses possible.

### When Assessing Reliability, All Relevant Sources of Error Should Be Examined

Reliability pertains to consistency; scores on a measure are considered to be reliable if the person completing that measure would receive the same score when completing the measure again under similar circumstances if no learning occurred since the first administration. Lack of consistency in scores stems from measurement error, and error can stem from a variety of potential sources, depending on the format of the assessment. Some measures, for instance, rely on teachers or others to rate students' behaviors or work products, and differences in how these raters apply the rating rules are one source of measurement error. The growth of performance assessment in the achievement domain has been accompanied by advances in research on statistical methods for identifying the magnitudes of errors stemming from different sources, and many of these methods have applications in the domains of interpersonal and intrapersonal competencies.

One interviewee told us that the most important area of research in score reliability today is the use of automated scoring that could increase efficiency and decrease costs for measures that are used on a large scale. The growth of technology-based formats not only makes automated scoring more feasible than it has been in the past but also permits examinees and scorers to access the testing materials remotely. So this is a topic that might be worthy of particular attention, along with the concomitant concerns associated with assessment and data security that could threaten the validity and reliability of scores, as well as the confidentiality of student information.

### Developers Should Ensure That New Measures Are Fair to Members of Different Groups

Fairness is often considered as it pertains to members of different racial, ethnic, or gender groups, but different measurement contexts raise different concerns about fairness. The West Point grit example described earlier illustrates this point: Is the measure fair if it results in lower scores for students in certain environments than in others solely because of the ways in which one's peer group influence one's responses? Research is needed not only to examine fairness but also to help developers design measures that will be fair and unbiased from the outset, such as through the universal-design approach that is sometimes applied to address the needs of students with disabilities. One advantage of this approach is to minimize the need to alter the measure or administration conditions after a measure has been developed.

### Technical Quality Should Be Considered When Making Choices Among Formats

As discussed earlier, the heavy reliance on self-report measures raises some concerns about the appropriateness of these measures for certain uses. Technical quality investigations can inform decisions about whether the self-report format might work in certain circumstances or whether the measure should rely on another, possibly more costly, approach. As one interviewee stated,

> I think what needs to happen in the field is to determine the appropriate balance of cost, ease, reliability, and validity. Right now, many of the assessments in these areas rely on Likert scales, self-reporting and personality type inventories and less on behavioral measures. There is a big concern about how much we should rely on these measures . . . versus behavioral indices that we could observe that might be more costly but might have greater validity.

Research on the validity, reliability, and fairness of scores on these different formats can be informative, along with comparisons among the different formats to determine the extent to which they produce consistent information.

### Technical Quality Investigations Should Examine Differences in How Measures Function in Different Contexts

Earlier, we discussed the importance of identifying when a construct might be considered stable or generalizable across different contexts and when it might be context dependent. For example, does a measure of collaboration that is shown to work well in a traditional high school function similarly in a more specialized high-school environment? Research on validity, reliability, and fairness should examine the context dependency of measures, and users of that research should recognize the extent to which it might be limited to a specific context and therefore largely uninformative about the measure's quality when used in a very different context.

### There Is a Need to Set Priorities Among Various Aspects of Technical Quality, Particularly When Resources to Investigate Quality Are Limited

Validity, reliability, and fairness each encompass a range of considerations, and the task of gathering evidence about all of them can seem daunting. For example, within the category of fairness, test users are advised to consider such issues as the ways in which test content might influence motivation or engagement differently depending on one's cultural background, the types of accommodations needed to ensure that examinees can perform to the best of their ability on a test, and the ways in which scoring rubrics might threaten the comparability of measurement across groups. Attending to the large number and diverse array of criteria provided in the standards document can seem overwhelming, particularly for developers and users who lack access to the kind of testing and data infrastructures on which large publishers can draw. It is important for developers and users to identify the criteria that are most relevant to a particular type of measure and to the contexts in which the measure is being used, while recognizing that the necessary criteria might change over time as the measure gets adopted in new contexts and as data from the measure are accumulated.

Evidence of the highest level of technical quality is essential for measures that are used for high-stakes purposes, which is one reason many of our interviewees indicated opposition to attaching stakes to interpersonal and intrapersonal competency measures. These interviewees noted that the evidence to support such uses is not close to the level that would support high-stakes use. At the same time, many expressed concerns about setting unrealistic expectations for quality of measures that are used primarily in a formative way and that, while some evidence needs to be gathered to support formative uses, it does not generally need to be as extensive as what would be expected for high-stakes uses.

### Newer Item Formats and Reporting Systems Might Require New Approaches to Assessing Technical Quality

As we noted earlier, advances in information technology have contributed to the development of innovative assessment formats across a range of disciplines and contexts. These new formats include, for example, simulations that allow respondents to interact with materials or avatars in ways that enable them to demonstrate their problem-solving and teamwork skills. These formats not only create a new kind of assessment experience for students; they also offer possibilities for more-comprehensive data, such as information about changing answers (revealed through tracking mouse clicks), the order in which students take various problem-solving steps, and time spent on specific screens. This information could be particularly valuable for studying such constructs as engagement, but the research on how to make sense of this information in the context of K–12 assessment is still in a very early phase. Research should be designed to help us understand how innovative assessment formats function, what the data tell us about students' competencies, and how educators might productively make use of this rich information to improve instruction and learning.

## Documenting Consequences of Assessment Use

Calls for the adoption of measures of interpersonal and intrapersonal competencies are often accompanied by claims about the benefits of using such measures. These potential benefits range from providing additional information to guide instructional decisions in the classroom to creating incentives for schools to emphasize a broader range of outcomes than they have in the past. At the same time, there are well-documented risks associated with the use of assessments. Although much of the policy debate around problems with achievement testing has focused on high-stakes uses of those tests, even lower-stakes uses can lead to unanticipated and undesirable consequences. Users of assessments should be clear on what outcomes they expect and should monitor the consequences of assessment use so that they can take steps to maximize the benefits and minimize harms. There is a lack of existing evidence regarding the consequences of measuring interpersonal and intrapersonal competencies at the K–12 level, so researchers and other stakeholders should consider ways to gather solid evidence of consequences when these assessments are being developed and on an ongoing basis once they are implemented in the field.

### Researchers Should Develop Guidance for Monitoring the Consequences of Assessment Use

Assessment users could benefit from clear guidance regarding methods for examining consequences at multiple levels—individual students, classrooms, schools, and broader systems. A variety of data-collection activities might be appropriate, depending on the nature of the assessment and the purpose for which it is being administered. For example, for an assessment that is intended to help teachers identify classroom-based interventions to address students' needs in the areas of intrapersonal competencies, it would be important to gather information from teachers about the perceived utility of the assessment for that purpose and about the specific interventions that they adopt. It would also be important to follow students over time to assess whether the interventions are appropriate and lead to desired outcomes. Failure to document these kinds of benefits should not necessarily be considered evidence that the use of the assessment is inappropriate or unhelpful, but it should prompt further exploration of how to make the best use of assessment results. Researchers could develop broad guidelines for data-collection strategies that are suited to several categories of use (e.g., instructional feedback, postsecondary admissions).

### High-Stakes Uses of Measures Require Research-Based Evidence That Is Likely to Be Expensive and Time-Consuming to Collect

As noted in the section on technical quality, high-stakes uses require the most-extensive evidence regarding validity, reliability, and fairness, and those who wish to use measures under high-stakes conditions should partner with researchers who can gather that evidence and provide guidance regarding appropriate use while the evidence is still being collected. Similarly, high-stakes uses also require careful monitoring of consequences, particularly given the likelihood that higher stakes could lead to manipulation, to unintended narrowing of instruction or curriculum, or to decisions about students that result in inequities across different groups (Koretz, 2008; Hamilton et al., 2013).

### Even Formative Uses of Measures Should Be Justified with Appropriate Evidence

Although we tend to worry less about undesirable consequences stemming from purely formative uses of measures than we do with high-stakes, summative uses, the widespread claims that formative assessment is beneficial for teaching and learning warrant careful investigation of whether those benefits are achieved. Several meeting participants and interviewees identified ways in which measures of interpersonal and intrapersonal competencies might be used by educators to improve student outcomes, such as this:

> These assessments ought to be used to help students learn from these assessments about themselves and the gap between what they know and what they need to know. Teachers need to understand the skill gaps of their students and how to change instruction to better prepare students.

There is some research evidence that points to the power of interventions to improve students' performance on some competencies, and research should continue to build on this work with a focus on understanding how interventions are adopted in schools and classrooms and what factors influence the kinds of responses that they promote. Studies should be designed around specific claims, such as the idea that teachers who have access to good measures will be able to personalize interventions to address individual students' needs.

In addition, although there was near consensus among participants that high-stakes uses are generally inappropriate, a few interviewees pointed out that a lack of consequences attached to measures of these competencies could result in educators paying less attention to them, particularly if those educators experience pressure to focus on high-stakes outcomes, such as test scores in mathematics and reading. One interviewee said,

> At the state and district levels, I would like to see meaningful metrics as a part of a system of accountability. I worry that, if these assessments are formative only, then they don't count in the system of accountability. These types of assessments provide deep

and rich information, but they also need to count as a component of a dashboard of measurements to monitor student learning.

Thus, although extreme caution is warranted when considering attaching stakes to measures, it is also important to monitor whether lower-stakes use is adequate to create the type of incentive environment that will ultimately lead the education system to broaden its focus to include these important constructs.

### Educators Should Receive Professional Development to Become Better Users of New Measures, and the Quality of the Professional Development Should Be Monitored

Several participants acknowledged the need to provide assessment users with professional development (PD) to help them make effective use of the information from new measures of interpersonal and intrapersonal competencies. One interviewee noted, "We need to be thinking about improving assessment literacy. That is, we need to pay more attention to building the capacity of school leaders' understanding of performance-based assessments." This interviewee, along with several others, also pointed out the need to help teachers embed the use of assessments into their classroom practices in a way that allows them to incorporate them into their teaching and address students' needs in their day-to-day instruction. Because many teachers and school leaders lack experience with interventions or assessments in this area, high-quality PD is likely to be a crucial component of any effort to promote a focus on interpersonal and intrapersonal competencies. However, evidence of PD's effectiveness in general K–12 settings suggests that much of the PD that is provided to educators does not contribute to effective, sustained instructional change (Garet et al., 2011). Research should build on what we know about the factors that contribute to effective PD and examine whether various approaches to PD are helpful for promoting the desired outcomes.

CHAPTER FOUR

# Promoting High-Quality Measures: Recommendations and Challenges

The meeting participants and interview respondents represented a wide variety of perspectives, and they differed in their specific recommendations for how to foster high-quality research and development of measures of interpersonal and intrapersonal competencies. Yet they largely agreed that the topic warrants a comprehensive, collaborative approach that brings together members of several different stakeholder groups and that considers both short-term and long-term objectives. The material presented in the previous chapters covers a variety of topics, and members of various stakeholder groups (e.g., researchers, practitioners) are likely to find some of the topics more directly relevant to their own work than others.

In this chapter, we focus on funders and policymakers, who are likely to play a significant role in setting and guiding the research and development agenda. As we described at the outset, we think that the process should be designed to promote the thoughtful development of practical, high-quality measures of interpersonal and intrapersonal competencies that practitioners and policymakers can use appropriately to improve valued outcomes for students. To advance these objectives, funders and policymakers would benefit from a strategic plan that encourages assessment development and identifies the resources and policy changes needed to support the development and use of new assessments. In this chapter, we identify some key questions that funders need to address, and we suggest a strategy that funders and policymakers might adopt to encourage and support the work of researchers, assessment developers, and the practitioners who use assessments.

Finally, we describe some of the challenges that are likely to arise even if the funding community follows this strategy.

## Recommendations for Promoting High-Quality Measures of Interpersonal and Intrapersonal Competencies

To support the development of new measures, Hewlett and its partners will have to answer certain questions, including the following:

- Which competencies should be addressed first?
- Which research and development goals should receive priority for the identified competencies?
- How long will the research and development process take, and how much money needs to be committed to support the efforts?
- How should the measurement-development process be managed?
  - How should individuals or organizations be selected to conduct the research and development?
  - How should the work of the developers be monitored?
  - What role should other constituents (e.g., policymakers, practitioners) play in the process, and how should they be informed?

Although we cannot answer all of these questions based on the work we have done, we can suggest a general strategy and, in some cases, offer tentative answers based on expert feedback from the meetings and interviews.

### Which Competencies Should Be Addressed First?

An informed answer to this question requires some additional research to understand what measures currently exist across the domains of interest; how good they are from a technical, as well as a practical, perspective; how difficult it is likely to be to develop new measures; and how beneficial the new measures are likely to be for practitioners. Before we discuss these points, it is worth noting that many of the participants at the meetings favored beginning with interpersonal competencies (such as communication or collaboration) in order to produce early successes. They felt that intrapersonal competencies, such as learning to learn, would pose greater measurement challenges and should be deferred until later in the process. However, this view was far from universal.

We think that the process of setting priorities among competencies should be guided by two main factors: how adequate the existing measures are for the intended purpose, and how difficult it is likely to be to develop new ones. Adequacy is a judgment based on the number of existing measures, their practicality for use by educators, and their technical quality vis-à-vis their intended purposes. Difficulty of development is a judgment based on researchers' depth understanding of the construct and familiarity with strategies for measuring it. The set of choices can be shown graphically as a two-dimensional grid in which the location of each competency area is determined by the adequacy of existing measures and the difficulty of developing new measures. Figure 4.1 shows what this arrangement might look like, using our sense of where three different competencies would be located.

**Figure 4.1**
**Adequacy and Difficulty of Measuring Selected Competencies**

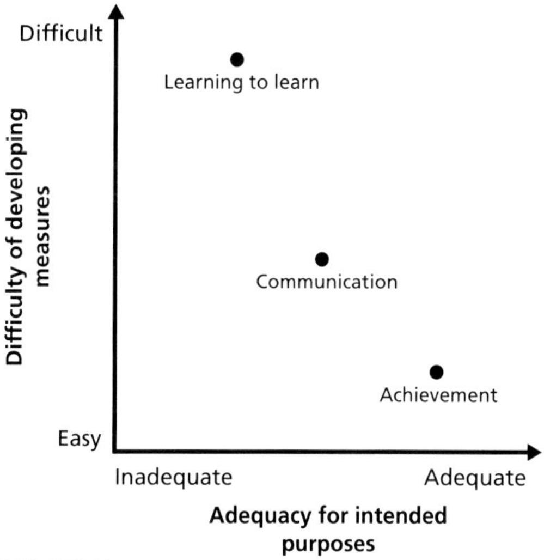


RAND *RR863-4.1*

If the figure were filled out for a wider range of competencies, then funders would have a more informed basis for deciding where to target their efforts. If they chose to follow the suggestions of many of the experts, they would look for competencies that had fewer measures and where development was likely to be not too difficult. The experts who suggested focusing on such low-hanging fruit pointed to competencies that are manifest in observable behaviors, e.g., in the interpersonal domain.

It is also essential that developers and funders consider the educational efficacy of the selected constructs. As noted earlier, by *educational efficacy,* we mean the extent to which the construct is malleable and likely to be influenced by interventions and the extent to which educators and others who are concerned about student outcomes view the construct as relevant and important.

### Which Research and Development Goals Should Receive Priority for the Identified Competencies?

We would recommend a second analytic step before making specific investments. This step involves consideration of the nature of the measurement gaps that exist. There are four kinds of activities that might be pursued: (1) conduct basic research to understand the nature of the psychological processes or behavioral manifestations that underlie a construct, (2) develop new measures for a construct that is well understood, (3) assess or improve the quality of an existing measure of a construct, or (4) investigate the consequences of educators using a measure in the school context. An interviewee explained the need for basic research on some competencies thusly:

> We do not understand much about how these competencies are built, how they are developed, and how they change by age and types of learning environments and level of prior knowledge. There are lots of questions we don't know the answer to. This is basic research, and we need to figure out how they connect with each other.

Our sense from talking with participants and interviewees is that there is still a need for basic research in the intrapersonal domain, which would be followed by efforts to address the other three goals. Although the interpersonal domain could also benefit from more basic research, it is our sense that these constructs are better understood than in the intrapersonal domain, so more of the initial effort could focus on measure development and then proceed to the other goals. In some cases, in which measures exist (for example, grit), more attention is needed on questions of quality and, once implemented in schools, on consequences. We would hope that ultimately we would have a balanced portfolio of research, with some investment in each of these types of research. However, to start, we would focus first on constructs in which some of the basic research has already been completed and there is room for more-immediate improvement in measures and their quality.

### How Long Will the Research and Development Process Take, and How Much Money Needs to Be Committed to Support the Efforts?

This question requires a different sort of analysis from the one we conducted. It would make sense to conduct a literature review and to consult with some commercial test developers to obtain more-realistic estimates for resource demands. One option to consider would be to conduct a competition and let the marketplace dictate the resource demands for a given competency.

It is also important to consider the time and resources that would be required to undertake the full set of development and evaluation activities recommended earlier in this report. To adequately evaluate validity, reliability, and fairness and to understand the consequences associated with operational use of a measure, a long-term and wide-ranging program of research is needed. This type of effort is probably not feasible for every measure but should be prioritized for those measures that are in widespread use or that are likely to be used under high-stakes conditions.

### How Should the Measurement-Development Process Be Managed?

The Hewlett Foundation and other philanthropic organizations have been pursuing their own individual initiatives related to interpersonal and intrapersonal competencies, and they recognize the limitations of this approach. The White House meeting was motivated in large part by a desire to coordinate their efforts and create greater momentum in this area.

We think the best way to muster resources and encourage a research and development agenda that is consistent with the goals we outlined is to create a pair of independent research-coordinating boards to guide the process, one for interpersonal competencies and the other for intrapersonal competencies. As one participant explained,

> A good example, not in education, is Bell Labs when they did fairly basic research. They took a long-run view of improving telephonic [and] electronic communication. They gave support to smart people, with a long-term horizon, keeping in the background that the point ultimately was to make money for AT&T.

The two boards would be made up of measurement and content experts and stakeholder representatives. Each board would create the research and development agenda, receive funding from contributing foundations and agencies, disburse it to developers, monitor the process incrementally, and make midcourse adjustments based on successes. The boards would not be responsible for doing the assessment-development or validation work. The funding community would provide resources that each board could contract for the needed tasks in its area of development. The boards should also have a multiple-year mandate to reflect that fact that the process of development and validation is likely to take multiple years and to help avoid the natural tendency for decisionmakers to move on to new initiatives before giving current initiatives a chance to prove their worth.

One advantage of this model is that it would foster collaboration in the development of the agenda rather than competition for resources. This is an important goal in the minds of many participants, as exemplified by this comment from an interview:

> Right now, funding is structured so that the person who is doing this research is incented to do work and make findings independently, rather than collaborating with the field. I think funding needs to be restructured to support collaboration, rather than just

> focusing on supporting individuals, so that we can understand what it is that we want to assess.

Another stated,

> We are people competing for the same set of funds, so if I [were] a funder, I wouldn't exacerbate that by picking winners and losers. We don't know what the winners and losers are; we should be focusing on collective brainpower.

Another advantage is that it could cast a wider net for evidence, including both domestic and international research, and examining research from school age through adulthood.

The process might involve the four steps described in the rest of this section.

#### *Establish Guidelines for the Operation of Research-Coordinating Boards*

The work of the coordinating board should be informed by clear guidelines that are designed not to restrict creativity but to establish expectations regarding the goals to achieve and likely intermediate steps. For example, the guidelines might suggest the following core tasks:

1. Conduct an environmental scan.
2. Develop a concept map showing how pieces related to one another.
3. Review the research base to clarify relationships among constructs and between constructs and outcomes.
4. Assemble a catalog of existing assessments detailing their approach, evidence of quality, practical considerations, potential uses, and other factors.
5. Identify key gaps in understanding.
6. Suggest priorities for new work.
7. Establish a rough timeline

These core tasks reflect important issues that participants identified.

Several interviewees urged this type of systematic approach to addressing development. For instance, one said,

> You have to know there are measures; you have to know what these measures are good for in a variety of contexts and populations and know what they should and shouldn't be used for. Think across the range of competencies you are trying to measure: What is the state of research in each, where are we . . . , what do we know, and ultimately go back and forth between theory and practice to figure out the best measures, and use the measures to push the theory.

The guidelines would also describe an operational model for how the center conducts business. For example, they might operate like a "portfolio school district" (Lake and Hill, 2009), which establishes goals, milestones, and measures of success, and then contracts with individual schools that assume the responsibility for allocating available resources to achieve them.

Dissemination should also be a focus of the board's work. As one interviewee noted,

> I'm dubious about how much more research needs to be done. There is more research that needs to be done, but how much of it is simply unpacking the research that has been done for decades? A lot of good research has been done, and peer-reviewed, but has not benefited from good packaging.

Highly accessible, user-friendly, and accurate information on measures and the research to support their use should be made widely available to potential users rather than published exclusively in limited-access venues, such as academic journals. Given the lack of funds and incentives for many researchers to do this type of publishing, the board could play an important role in ensuring that it happens.

#### *Select Initial Competencies and Develop Priorities for Research-Coordinating Board Efforts*

We suggest establishing one board to coordinate efforts related to interpersonal competencies and another for intrapersonal competencies.

This organization reflects comments from several participants, such as the following:

> I would think about creating a funding initiative with a larger plan and designed to include funding a collaborative or distributive center focused on a long-term agenda for accomplishing these goals supported by field-initiated work. I would not put it all in one center because it would not adequately represent the depth and breadth of the work that needs to be done.

We imagine that the boards would further subdivide their efforts into conceptually coherent chunks. Pellegrino and Hilton (2012) identifies clusters within the two broad competency areas that might be a sensible way for the boards to organize their planning. The authors identified two clusters within the interpersonal competencies of teamwork and collaboration and leadership and three clusters within the intrapersonal competencies of intellectual openness, work ethic and conscientiousness, and positive core self-evaluation. The idea of forming smaller, conceptually coherent subdivisions is consistent with suggestion from another interviewee, who said,

> It will be easier to achieve this by breaking the workshops [or] conferences out by competencies, starting with the low-hanging fruit. By starting with something easy and concrete, like oral communication, you can help people understand the process that will be used for the rest of the competency discussions.

Funders and policymakers need to reach some level of agreement on priorities for the initial investment in the boards. Reaching consensus is likely to be challenging, but an effort to identify priorities is crucial for informing funding decisions and for sending clear messages to the field that will encourage scholars to put their energies into efforts that will be most productive. Also, as one meeting participant pointed out, "we cannot develop assessments in all . . . domains [that we discussed] because it isn't practical in the current environment. We need to prioritize on things that are the most important." This prioritization should be informed, at least in part, by consideration of the adequacy of existing measures and the difficulty of developing new ones, as suggested above. Funders and policymakers might also want to take into account the current and projected future needs of practitioners, as well as the capacity of existing research teams to launch a comprehensive research and development agenda relatively quickly.

Setting priorities could help ensure that important steps in the research and development process are not skipped because of a lack of funds or researcher interest in those steps. For instance, as noted above, construct mapping is an important step. Several meeting participants and interviewees identified a need for a construct-mapping and definition step: e.g., "One of the first issues . . . is to fund individuals to try to bring clarity to the range of so-called constructs that fall into these domains. There are lots of terms and labels and many share similarities." Another noted,

> For each construct, there are so many different ideas of what it means and so many different ways to measure it. The opportunities for people to talk across different projects, so that there is clarity over how people contextualize [and] measure things differently; move towards consensus towards mapping out each construct.

Participants also pointed out the value of basic research, and it is important to decide whether this falls under the purview of the research-coordinating boards. Existing sources of funding do not necessarily support this type of research, but the boards may feel that it is essential to develop basic knowledge to support new measures. One interviewee expressed concern that practitioners' desires for quick answers often drives researchers' and developers' decisions about what to focus on, leading to applied research that can sometimes come at the expense of necessary basic research.

#### *Obtain Commitments for Multiple-Year Funding*

The comprehensive, sustained research that interview and meeting participants argued is needed requires researchers to have access to a funding source that can support that type of work. Funders and policymakers should collaborate to create a pool of resources to be made available to each center to operate for a minimum of five years, with annual or biennial reviews of progress. As noted by one interviewee, "I would think about creating a funding initiative with a larger plan and designed to include funding a collaborative or distributive center focused on a long-term agenda for accomplishing these goals supported by field-initiated work." As we discussed above, this type of multiple-year program of research is particularly important for measures that are likely to be used widely and for high-stakes purposes. This type of effort might benefit from collaboration among government agencies and nonprofit and for-profit organizations. There are some existing examples that could serve as models, such as the National Science Foundation's (NSF's) collaboration with the Bill & Melinda Gates Foundation on the Basic Research to Enable Agricultural Development (BREAD) program and its partnership with Intel and General Electric on an initiative to increase the number of engineers and computer scientists in the United States (NSF, undated, 2013).

#### *Appoint Representatives from Relevant Stakeholder Groups and Disciplines to Serve on the Research-Coordinating Boards*

A persistent theme in our conversations centered on the need to engage scholars who come from a variety of disciplines and intellectual traditions, including but not limited to traditional measurement and psychology researchers. As one interviewee suggested,

> Pick the top eight to ten researchers; give them some money. Give them nine to 12 [months] to figure out how they can work collaboratively. At the end, as a group, have them decide where the agenda could go, who would be best at what, where their work overlaps.

In addition to disciplinary diversity among researchers, the effort should engage those who represent groups that are likely to contribute to the development and use of new measures. Input from educators is crucial, particularly classroom teachers who will be on the front lines of making use of information from new measures. Employers are another important group that should be involved in the research boards. An interviewee noted the importance of encouraging research–

practitioner collaborations: "Tell the researchers to take the practitioners seriously and listen to them and be respectful and then make some of the funding dependent on that." Nonprofit organizations represent another important constituency. As one representative from a nonprofit group noted, "We're very open to partnering with researchers. I see us as pushing people to take action and move quickly and as partners for the research work." Commercial publishers and other for-profit companies are also likely to play an important role in administering and maintaining measures once they are deployed in the field.

## Remaining Challenges

The measurement-development process could flounder for a variety of reasons, and a careful hand will be needed on the tiller to ensure its success. Participants in the meetings and interviews identified some potential pitfalls and problems, described in this section.

### Reaching Consensus Among Funders on Where to Focus the Efforts

It is likely to be difficult to obtain consensus on priorities among funders and policymakers. Even within our relatively small sample, we heard multiple perspectives on how the research should be carried out. For example, some preferred a diffuse model:

> The conceptual framework is "We don't know a lot. So we have to try a lot of things." I would try to get a lot of different people to do a lot of different things. It is better to make reasonable starts on a number of projects than making heavy bets on a few projects.

Others wanted to see more concentration:

> At the White House conference, it became apparent that there are too many people working with too little capacity to actually do significant work in assessment, and they're going to need to figure out how to set priorities and make choices about where to more narrowly focus efforts.

Moreover, there may be incentives for individual organizations to emphasize their own unique approaches. One interviewee noted,

> Hewlett is tied to deeper learning, MacArthur [Foundation] to connected learning, Gates to next-generation learning. From a branding standpoint, organizations need ownership of these concepts and ideas. But it is important to let go of ego; to advance this work, we need a better sense of the nomenclature.

The funders will have to watch the process to be sure that the boards are able to maintain a collaborative focus.

### Maintaining Standards for Rigor of the Measures

Given the growing interest in measuring interpersonal and intrapersonal competencies for various purposes, such as postsecondary planning and school accountability, researchers and developers are likely to feel pressure to produce assessments rapidly and deploy them widely, perhaps before the assessments are ready and before anyone has a good understanding of how the use of such measures can improve outcomes for students. As one of the participants warned,

> People compare this to the self-esteem movement. I have repeatedly heard people say, "We don't want to go the way of the self-esteem movement. We want to really understand what we're doing before we start promoting it on a wide scale, whatever 'it' is." . . . When we're out there with ideas that are not clearly defined, or not well understood, . . . we end up promoting bad practice.

There will be pressures to release measures quickly, but care must be taken to stay with research until quality is ensured.

### Generating Public Support and Maintaining Policymaker Interest in the Measures

The difficult rollout of the Common Core State Standards illustrates some of the risks associated with trying to create public and political buy-in for education reforms that are voluntary, are perceived as threatening local control, or have become overly politicized. Our participants noted the significant risk of pushback from parents or others who worry about potential negative effects of measuring these nonacademic outcomes, including potential misuse of data. As one participant noted, "You have got to create a public policy environment in which people—policymakers, practitioners, the informed public—believe [that] this is an issue worth attending to." One interviewee suggested that the key to getting policymaker support is developing

> a narrative or a theory of action that connects the investment in research to some outcomes that policymakers care about. For example, let's say that we know how to not only measure what constitutes a growth mind-set, but we have research that shows that getting people to believe [that] the growth mind-set has the following impact on academic outcomes. And that it's possible to deliver the growth mind-set intervention in an online way so that it's scalable. . . . And we've done enough research to show that delivering the growth mind-set has an impact on student learning outcomes. People would go, "Yeah, maybe we should do more in the area of growth mind-set."

Others pointed to concerns about maintaining public support:

> There's a big risk, politically, in getting ahead of oneself with this stuff because there are natural critics of this work who, if you don't manage the public rollout effectively, will pounce on it and undermine it.

We were reminded that this discussion is occurring in the context of two expensive new assessment systems (the Smarter Balanced Assessment System and the Partnership for Assessment of Readiness for College and Careers [PARCC]), and "it is not clear [whether] there will be support for additional new assessments." Funders and policymakers must recognize the importance of taking local needs and interests into account: "You can't drive reform from the federal or state level. You can set parameters, provide resources, and hold people accountable, but you need to recognize that the people on the ground understand their needs better than people higher up."

### Staying the Course

It is a common complaint that policymakers move on to the next big thing before the initiatives that are currently being supported have had a chance to demonstrate their effectiveness. Efforts to expand measurement will certainly encounter setbacks and will almost certainly not lead to the promised benefits right away. And as discussed earlier in this report, many of the steps that need to be taken to ensure that measures are of high quality will take several years to carry out. Several interviewees raised this concern: "This is going to be a continuous improvement process that will take decades, and I have no sense of whether or not agencies will be willing to sustain their effort for that period of time." Another said,

> But high-quality measurement work is not fast, and there is a huge amount of work on the front end. . . . To do this well, we need to think about the building blocks, relationships, and what [it] means; this work is very hard [to sustain]. And it is not just policymakers who want quick results: Many foundations in the education space are very impatient, in part because they have conceptualized their work to be very strategic, so they want fast outcomes. This is being encouraged by the Department of Education; [it wants] things very fast.

It is essential that those who are setting the agenda manage the expectations of policymakers, funders, practitioners, and others who understandably are looking for quick-turnaround studies and for tools they can use right away.

### Sustaining a Collaborative Culture

Our proposed strategy emphasizes collaboration to address the complex, multidisciplinary nature of the proposed research. But developing and sustaining long-term collaborative efforts is challenging, especially in light of the incentives that many researchers face to demonstrate a track record of grants or publications that might be easier to achieve in a less collaborative context. One interviewee said,

> Right now, there are a lot of us in this field, stepping on each other's toes. We use different terms, but they are roughly the same thing. If I was a funder, I would try to get some of the top people and try to get them to work collaboratively versus competitively. We are in this exploratory labeling phase. We are on the verge of people sniping at each other, because I call it mind-set versus persistence versus grit.

CHAPTER FIVE

# Conclusion

Researchers are demonstrating the importance of many interpersonal and intrapersonal competencies for success in college and careers. The Hewlett Foundation believes that better measurement of these competencies is necessary for schools to be able to support their development and that such measures can be important levers to improve public education for all students. This report describes a framework for a program of research and development to create and evaluate new measures of interpersonal and intrapersonal competencies, and it suggests one strategy that could be followed to bring resources to bear on the measurement challenge in an efficient manner. Regardless of whether this specific approach is adopted, it is clear that the development of new measures offers promise, as well as pitfalls, and that it will require participation from members of all of the groups that will be affected by this effort: researchers, policymakers, educational practitioners, and students. Funders have a crucial role to play in bringing these groups together and promoting a sustained, long-term research and development agenda that will not be derailed by short-term political and practical constraints. Although there are many examples of individual foundations and individual government agencies that have sponsored sustained programs of research of the type suggested here, there are few examples of collaboration among these organizations to achieve a shared objective, such as the development of measures of interpersonal and intrapersonal competencies. There appears to be momentum to make that happen, and we hope that it is enough to create a community of interest to advance this agenda.

APPENDIX A

# Summary of the White House Workshop on Hard-to-Measure 21st-Century Skills

*February 3, 2014; distributed to participants in March 2014 and lightly edited here*

It has been about a month since a select group of researchers, policymakers, practitioners, and funders gathered in the White House Conference Center to discuss the assessment of *academic mind-sets, collaboration, oral communication, learning to learn*, and other hard-to-measure 21st-century competencies. This note summarizes the highlights of those discussions, both to keep the ideas current in your minds and to build momentum for action to address the challenges that were identified in the areas of research, funding, and policymaking.

## Where Did We Start?

Five papers were circulated prior to the workshop, which sought to establish the following:

- the need for promoting 21st-century competencies to better equip students for work and life in a globalized world
- the current status of assessment of 21st-century competencies—an eclectic mix of research and commercial products addressing a diverse but uneven set of competencies
- a new vision for assessment that puts greater emphasis on assessments *for* learning than assessment *of* learning and encourages us to think about systems of assessment rather than individual tests.

## What Opening Challenges Were Posed?

Lisa Petrides of the Institute for the Study of Knowledge Management in Education (ISKME) offered a structure for thinking about the challenges that make these competencies "hard to measure" and "hard to incorporate" into educational systems. We must find ways to address

- technical challenges related to measurement (including reliability, validity, and fairness)
- implementation challenges (e.g., scale-up, cost, timing)
- political challenges (creating new policies and mustering the political will to adopt them)
- public-acceptance challenges (educating the general public and mustering its support for change).

Thomas W. Brock of the National Center for Education Research (NCER) highlighted three needs:

- semantic—the need to clarify how we describe these domains, so policymakers, practitioners, and the public will understand the distinctions among the domains and each domain's relevance to schooling
- teaching and learning—the need to figure out how, where, and when students should learn these competencies as part of their education
- assessment—the need to incorporate assessments into classrooms; since teachers and students are feeling bombarded with testing demands, there is a need to make the assessments meaningful and useful to students and teachers in the immediate future, as well as the long term.

Joan Ferrini-Mundy of NSF discussed NSF's interest in deeper learning in the context of the STEM disciplines, as well as workforce training in these disciplines. She highlighted the need to focus on the complex interplay between subject-specific expertise and general competencies and to attend to the developmental trajectory of these competencies—how do they manifest themselves from first through

12th grades? She also noted the value of planned interdisciplinary research that is contributing to the development of our understanding (e.g., computer scientists who think about use of data, engineers who think about how students learn engineering principles, mathematicians who do work in modeling and algorithms).

Roberto Rodríguez, special assistant to the President for education policy, pushed us to move from thinking about schools as a place where students passively receive knowledge and skills to a place where learning is student-centered, personalized, and engaging. This change requires addressing three challenges:

- The lack of a *pedagogical road map and curricula* to foster these skills and competencies and put students on a path to college- and career-ready standards. We need to do more to support and provide tools for educators to promote development of these skills in a more deliberate way.
- The lack of the *policy architecture* and scale to bring to bear better assessment of these skills. Measures exist, but the challenge is how to think about assessment as an important piece that undergirds states' efforts to implement new standardized assessments of skills related to college and career readiness.
- The lack of knowledge of how to *support teachers*, to foster 21st-century skills, both in classroom and in other places where youth spend time: e.g., libraries, community centers.

All the challenges that were raised in these introductory presentations would continue to be the subject of discussion for the remainder of the day.

## What Ideas Were Discussed?

The rest of the morning was spent in small-group discussions of what is known about measuring these skills, teaching these skills, and the impact of these skills on later student outcomes. Here are some of the points that were made, organized in terms of the challenges identified in the opening remarks:

- technical challenges
  - We need better definitions for these competencies.
  - There are a variety of ways researchers can better understand these constructs, including the use of expert practitioner knowledge, using computer-based assessment data (e.g., from the National Assessment of Educational Progress [NAEP]) to examine keystroke-level information, and looking at what practitioners and policymakers take these ideas to mean.
  - In thinking about the validity of new assessments, we should not forget the distinction between proximal indicators and long-term indicators of success.
  - States have pressing short-term needs for measures they can use, but we should not neglect the need to validate measures, a process that typically requires extensive evidence collection over a long period of time.
- implementation challenges
  - Within the research community, there are different components of work occurring (e.g., NSF, NAEP, researchers) that need to be coordinated. How do we connect such research with the needs of practice?
  - The burning need for assessment is at the local level, where there is a desire for feedback on practice; cross-school or cross-district comparisons are of less interest to most educators and practitioners.
  - There is a need to consider what can actually be taught and under what circumstances it can be taught.
- political challenges
  - There is a policy war going on about who is in charge of assessment—the federal government, state governments, or local entities, such as school districts. We need greater public engagement to help resolve this conflict.
  - Researchers and prospective users must recognize the centrality and complexity of assessments and the challenges presented by

limited state and local capacity. They must also attend to federal policies and the incentives that follow from them.
  - Are we developing measures of academic mind-sets (and other 21st-century competencies) in order to deepen academic content or to foster transferable skills?
- public-acceptance challenges
  - *Assessment* has negative connotations to many people; how can we move away from that conceptualization? For example, do video games or badges offer a new paradigm for thinking about assessment?
  - It is unfair to compare what we know about measuring cognitive content and metacognitive skills; educators have been working on the former for many decades.

Brandon Wiley of the Asia Society and Diane Tavenner of Summit Public Schools talked about innovative school-based assessments in use in specific schools. They described conditions that might facilitate or hinder effective use of information from assessments of hard-to-measure skills, offering a valuable practitioner perspective.

## Where Do We Go from Here?

During the afternoon, we identified issues for further study and collective effort, focusing on questions related to research, policymaking, and funding.

- Research: There is a need to develop a clear, comprehensive research agenda related to *academic mind-sets*, *collaboration*, *oral communication*, *learning to learn*, and other hard-to-measure 21st-century skills and competencies. One key challenge is to develop a better understanding of the content-relatedness of these skills and a clearer conception of competencies that manifest across subjects. Research also needs to provide better understanding of existing inequalities in access to experiences that would promote development of these competencies and the implications for assessment. We need to think innovatively about where and how to assess competencies and make sure that assessment-based judgments transfer from the assessment setting to the authentic situation about which we care (i.e., are valid for their intended purpose). In addition, there is a need for research that explores how teachers and others will integrate new assessments into their instruction and how the new vision for assessment will be transmitted through teacher preservice training and PD. The agenda should be guided by the need to improve practice and develop a functioning assessment system.

- Policy: Most participants agreed that the development of a collection of new assessments alone would not be sufficient; instead, we also need a new vision for the role of assessment that emphasizes learning over accountability. Any new assessment policy should place greater emphasis on formative assessment than on summative assessment. New policies are also needed to increase the capacity of teachers and others to use assessment information to improve student learning. We need to complete the development of learning progressions related to these 21st-century competencies. Policies should be implemented to help teachers better understand how to implement good formative assessments. Reporting systems are also ripe for improvement, and creative policies should be developed that encourage multiple indicators, allow state standardized tests to exist alongside other assessments, and support the development of student learning profiles and other methods that allow students to demonstrate proficiency in ways that are meaningful for them.
- Funding: No predictable source of funds currently exists to support the research and policy development efforts discussed above, but participants believe that funders could be engaged in partnerships that would enable such development, research, and innovation. Perhaps new kinds of collaborations are needed (like those of, e.g., precompetitive research and development efforts in industry, the interstate highway system, rural electrification, and the Common Core State Standards) to build relationships between organizations. Different kinds of funding are needed depending

on the status of research on a particular skill construct, ranging from proof of concept to design of interventions to scale-up. The goal should be stable, sustainable flow of funds across different public and private funders to support research on learning environments that promote 21st-century competencies. One might start with mapping and framing exercises to help funders see how this fits with their existing priorities (e.g., research, advocacy, direct service). It is important not to define the field so narrowly that funders see this as outside their interests.

## What Is Needed to Get There?

During conversations at the end of the meeting, we identified some next steps.

1. The Hewlett Foundation is organizing a follow-up meeting prior to the next AERA conference to continue the discussion, with a focus on developing a research agenda.
2. The foundation is also pursuing the idea of an online repository or wiki where relevant assessments and related evidence could be stored and made available to interested parties.
3. Some participants identified specific actions that they or their organizations would take to support these developments.
   a. Michele Cahill of the Carnegie Corporation of New York and Craig Wacker of the Raikes Foundation are working together to promote changes in practice related to these competencies.
   b. John Easton of the Institute of Education Sciences indicated that the Organisation for Economic Co-operation and Development (OECD) would conduct a large-scale survey relating to socioemotional and cognitive competencies.
   c. Terri Shuck and Daniel Leeds of the National Public Education Support Fund agreed to assemble a strategy group to meet to continue this discussion and to encourage their

organization's members to work with this group to further the agendas we discussed.

d. Camille Farrington of the University of Chicago is compiling evidence about the factors that matter in developing college and career readiness from early childhood onward.
e. Andrew Calkins of Next Generation Learning Challenges will conduct "deeper dives" in schools to identify effective practices to promote these competencies.

Other participants indicated their intentions to continue to promote these competencies through, e.g., focused research in schools, additional conversations, incorporating these ideas into future grantmaking, and exploring the development of these competencies in informal educational settings.

We also identified a couple of strategic needs, if this work is to be sustained effectively:

- To increase the likelihood that individual efforts on the part of researchers, policymakers, and funders achieve goals with respect to hard-to-measure 21st-century competencies, we need to develop a broad strategic plan to promote the development, review, implementation, and use of assessments. Such a strategic plan would identify short-term, intermediate-term, and long-term goals for research, policymaking, and funding; delineate steps to take to achieve these goals; identify interconnections among the three strands of work (research, policymaking, and funding); and develop milestones to monitor progress along the multiple pathways.
- To promote, support, and monitor progress toward the strategic goals, we should create a coordinating body with representative from key groups that will maintain the focus on the goals, assess progress, identify critical paths, set priorities, coordinate diverse groups needed to take the next steps, and marshal support from diverse constituencies that will be needed to make this happen.

APPENDIX B

# Experts Who Participated in Meetings and Interviews

The following people participated in the meetings or interviews (or both) that we have described in this report. The affiliations and positions listed here were current as of May 2014.

- Rachel Goldman Alper, director of strategic alliances, Maker Education Initiative, Washington, D.C.
- Maggie Barber, research analyst, ISKME, Half Moon Bay, California
- Gregg S. Behr, executive director, Grable Foundation, Pittsburgh, Pennsylvania
- Roger Benjamin, president, Council for Aid to Education (CAE), New York, New York
- Stephen Bowen, director of innovation, Council of Chief State School Officers (CCSSO), Washington, D.C.
- Jonathan Brice, Deputy Assistant Secretary for Policy, U.S. Department of Education, Washington, D.C.
- Eduardo Briceño, co-founder and CEO, Mindset Works, Walnut, California
- Thomas Brock, commissioner, Institute of Education Sciences, Washington, D.C.
- Christopher Brown, then director, Pearson Education, New York, New York
- Michele Cahill, vice president for national program and program director for urban education, Carnegie Corporation of New York, New York, New York

- Andrew Calkins, deputy director, Next Generation Learning Challenges, Gloucester, Massachusetts
- Barbara Chow, education program director, William and Flora Hewlett Foundation, Menlo Park, California
- Marc Chun, education program officer, William and Flora Hewlett Foundation, Menlo Park, California
- David Conley, CEO, Educational Policy Improvement Center (EPIC), Eugene, Oregon
- Seth Corrigan, director of education and evaluation, GlassLab, Redwood City, California
- Linda Darling-Hammond, professor and codirector, School Redesign Network (SRN), Stanford University, Stanford, California
- Deborah S. Delisle, Assistant Secretary for Elementary and Secondary Education, U.S. Department of Education, Washington, D.C.
- Angela Duckworth, associate professor, University of Pennsylvania, Philadelphia, Pennsylvania
- Richard A. Duschl, division director, NSF, Arlington, Virginia
- Carol S. Dweck, Lewis and Virginia Eaton Professor of Psychology, Stanford University, Stanford, California
- Janice M. Earle, program director, NSF, Arlington, Virginia
- John Easton, director, Institute of Education Sciences, Washington, D.C.
- Charles Fadel, founder and chair, Center for Curriculum Redesign, Boston, Massachusetts
- Camille A. Farrington, assistant professor, University of Chicago, Chicago, Illinois
- Joan Ferrini-Mundy, assistant director for education and human resources, NSF, Arlington, Virginia
- Kumar Garg, senior adviser to the deputy director, Office of Science and Technology Policy, Executive Office of the President, Washington, D.C.
- Laura S. Hamilton, senior behavioral scientist, RAND Corporation, Pittsburgh, Pennsylvania
- Rafael Heller, principal policy analyst, Jobs for the Future, Washington, D.C.

- Andrés Henríquez, program director, NSF, Arlington, Virginia
- Kathleen E. Herbek, confidential assistant, Executive Office of the President, Washington, D.C.
- Joan Herman, codirector emeritus, National Center for Research on Evaluation, Standards, and Student Testing (CRESST), University of California Los Angeles, Los Angeles, California
- Diana E. Hess, senior vice president, Spencer Foundation, Chicago, Illinois
- Margaret Hilton, senior program officer, NRC, Washington, D.C.
- Cynthia Jimes, director of research, ISKME, Half Moon Bay, California
- Thomas Kalil, deputy director for technology and innovation, Office of Science and Technology Policy, Executive Office of the President, Washington, D.C.
- Kimberly T. Kendziora, principal researcher, American Institutes for Research (AIR), Washington, D.C.
- Michael Kubiak, chief research and evaluation officer, Citizen Schools, Cambridge, Massachusetts
- Paul Leather, deputy commissioner of education, New Hampshire Department of Education, Concord, New Hampshire
- Daniel Leeds, founder and president, National Public Education Support Fund, Washington, D.C.
- Andrew Maul, assistant professor, research and evaluation methodology, University of Colorado Boulder
- Merrilea Mayo, founder, Mayo Enterprises, North Potomac, Maryland
- Camsie McAdams, senior adviser on STEM education, Executive Office of the President, Washington, D.C.
- Michael S. McPherson, president, Spencer Foundation, Chicago, Illinois
- Vicki Myers, special assistant, U.S. Department of Education, Washington, D.C.
- Jennifer O'Day, managing research scientist, AIR, San Mateo, California

- Andreas Oranje, director of statistical analysis, ETS, San Francisco, California
- Cornelia Orr, executive director, National Assessment Governing Board, Washington, D.C.
- Steven Paine, president, Partnership for 21st Century Skills, Washington, D.C.
- Randy Paris, confidential assistant, Office of Science and Technology Policy, Executive Office of the President, Washington, D.C.
- Dave Paunesku, graduate research fellow, Project for Education Research That Scales (PERTS), Stanford University, Stanford, California
- Ray Pecheone, executive director, Stanford Center for Assessment, Learning, and Equity (SCALE), Stanford University, Stanford, California
- James W. Pellegrino, professor and director of Learning Sciences Research Institute, University of Illinois at Chicago, Chicago, Illinois
- Lisa Petrides, president and founder, ISKME, Half Moon Bay, California
- Jonathan Plucker, professor of education, University of Connecticut, Storrs, Connecticut
- Sanjiv Rao, program officer, Ford Foundation, New York, New York
- Hilary Rhodes, senior research and evaluation officer, Wallace Foundation, New York, New York
- Roberto Rodríguez, special assistant to the President for education policy, Executive Office of the President, Washington, D.C.
- Carissa Romero, associate director, PERTS, Stanford University, Stanford, California
- Jody Rosentswieg, program officer, Raikes Foundation, Seattle, Washington
- Scott Sargrad, Deputy Assistant Secretary for Policy and Strategic Initiatives, U.S. Department of Education, Washington, D.C.

- Maya Shankar, senior adviser to the Deputy Director Social and Behavioral Sciences, Office of Science Technology and Policy, Washington, D.C.
- Christopher Shearer, education program officer, William and Flora Hewlett Foundation, Menlo Park, California
- Terri Shuck, executive director, National Public Education Support Fund, Washington, D.C.
- Susan R. Singer, division director, NSF, Arlington, Virginia
- Emily Dalton Smith, program officer, Next Generation Learning Challenges, Bill & Melinda Gates Foundation, Washington, D.C.
- Jonathan Snyder, executive director, Stanford Center for Opportunity Policy in Education, Stanford, California
- Helen Soule, executive director, Partnership for 21st Century Skills, Washington, D.C.
- Brian M. Stecher, associate director, RAND Education, RAND Corporation, Santa Monica, California
- Diane Tavenner, founder and CEO, Summit Public Schools, Redwood City, California
- James Taylor, principal researcher, Education Program, AIR, Washington, D.C.
- Stephanie Teasley, research professor, University of Michigan School of Information, Ann Arbor, Michigan
- Thomas Toch, senior managing partner and director of the Washington office, Carnegie Foundation for the Advancement of Teaching, Washington, D.C.
- Vivian Tseng, program officer, William T. Grant Foundation, New York, New York
- Denis Udall, education program officer, William and Flora Hewlett Foundation, Menlo Park, California
- Craig Wacker, program officer, Raikes Foundation, Seattle, Washington
- Phoenix Wang, principal partner, J Nowak and Associates, Philadelphia, Pennsylvania
- Joanne Weiss, former chief of staff for the U.S. Secretary of Education, Washington, D.C.

- Brandon Wiley, director, International Studies Schools Network, Asia Society, New York, New York
- Rebecca E. Wolfe, director, Students at the Center, Jobs for the Future, Washington, D.C.
- David Yeager, assistant professor, University of Texas at Austin, Austin, Texas.

# References


American Educational Research Association, American Psychological Association, and National Council on Measurement in Education, *Standards for Educational and Psychological Testing*, Washington, D.C.: American Educational Research Association, 2014.

Blackwell, Lisa S., Kali H. Trzesniewski, and Carol Sorich Dweck, "Implicit Theories of Intelligence Predict Achievement Across an Adolescent Transition: A Longitudinal Study and an Intervention," *Child Development*, Vol. 78, No. 1, January–February 2007, pp. 246–263.

Cohen, Geoffrey L., Julio Garcia, Nancy Apfel, and Allison Master, "Reducing the Racial Achievement Gap: A Social-Psychological Intervention," *Science*, Vol. 313, No. 5791, September 1, 2006, pp. 1307–1310.

Conley, David T., "New Conceptions of College and Career Ready: A Profile Approach to Admission," *Journal of College Admission*, No. 223, April 2014, pp. 12–23.

Cramond, Bonnie, Juanita Matthews-Morgan, Deborah Bandalos, and Li Zuo, "A Report on the 40-Year Follow-Up of the Torrance Tests of Creative Thinking: Alive and Well in the New Millennium," *Gifted Child Quarterly*, Vol. 49, No. 4, Fall 2005, pp. 283–291.

Duckworth, Angela Lee, personal communication with the authors, 2014.

Duckworth, Angela Lee, Christopher Peterson, Michael D. Matthews, and Dennis R. Kelly, "Grit: Perseverance and Passion for Long-Term Goals," *Journal of Personality and Social Psychology*, Vol. 92, No. 6, 2007, pp. 1087–1101.

Duckworth, Angela Lee, and Patrick D. Quinn, "Development and Validation of the Short Grit Scale (Grit-S)," *Journal of Personality Assessment*, Vol. 91, No. 2, 2009, pp. 166–174.

Dweck, Carol S., Gregory M. Walton, and Geoffrey L. Cohen, "Academic Tenacity: Mindsets and Skills That Promote Long-Term Learning," Bill and Melinda Gates Foundation, January 28, 2014. As of October 1, 2014: http://collegeready.gatesfoundation.org/article/academic-tenacity-mindsets-and-skills-promote-long-term-learning

Educational Testing Service, "How Tests and Test Questions Are Developed," undated; referenced March 14, 2014. As of October 12, 2014: https://www.ets.org/understanding_testing/test_development

Farrington, Camille A., Melissa Roderick, Elaine Allensworth, Jenny Nagaoka, Tasha Seneca Keyes, David W. Johnson, and Nicole O. Beechum, *Teaching Adolescents to Become Learners: The Role of Noncognitive Factors in Shaping School Performance—A Critical Literature Review*, Chicago, Ill.: Consortium on Chicago School Research, 2012. As of October 1, 2014: http://bibpurl.oclc.org/web/49257

Franken, Robert E. *Human Motivation*, 3rd ed., Pacific Grove, Ill.: Brooks/Cole, 1993.

Garet, Michael S., Andrew J. Wayne, Fran Stancavage, James Taylor, Marian Eaton, Kirk Walters, Mengli Song, Seth Brown, Steven Hurlburt, Pei Zhu, Susan Sepanik, Fred Doolittle, and Elizabeth Warner, *Middle School Mathematics Professional Development Impact Study: Findings After the Second Year of Implementation*, Washington, D.C.: National Center for Education Evaluation and Regional Assistance, Institute of Education Sciences, U.S. Department of Education, NCEE 2011-4024, 2011. As of October 1, 2014: http://purl.fdlp.gov/GPO/gpo13948

Goff, Kathy, and E. Paul Torrance, *Abbreviated Torrance Test for Adults*, Bensenville, Ill.: Scholastic Testing Service, 2002.

Griffin, Patrick E., personal communication with the authors, 2014.

Griffin, Patrick E., and Esther Care, "Project Method Overview," in Patrick Griffin and Esther Care, eds., *Assessment and Teaching of 21st Century Skills*, Vol. 2: *Methods and Approaches*, Dordrecht, the Netherlands: Springer, 2015.

Hamilton, Laura S., Heather L. Schwartz, Brian S. Stecher, and Jennifer L. Steele, "Improving Accountability Through Expanded Measures of Performance," *Journal of Educational Administration*, Vol. 51, No. 4, 2013, pp. 453–475.

Heckman, James J., "Schools, Skills, and Synapses," *Economic Inquiry*, Vol. 46, No. 3, July 2008, pp. 289–324.

Kane, Michael T., "Validation," in Robert L. Brennan, ed., *Educational Measurement*, 4th ed., Westport, Conn.: Praeger Publishers, 2006, pp. 17–64.

KIPP Schools, "Character Counts," undated. As of October 2, 2014: http://www.kipp.org/our-approach/character#sthash.01QC0XCi.dpuf

———, "Character Lab," January 2014. As of October 2, 2014:
http://www.kipp.org/files/dmfile/January2014CharacterGrowthCard.pdf

Koretz, Daniel M., *Measuring Up: What Educational Testing Really Tells Us*, Cambridge, Mass.: Harvard University Press, 2008.

Kyllonen, Patrick C., "Soft Skills for the Workplace," *Change*, November–December 2013; referenced July 30, 2014. As of October 1, 2014:
http://www.changemag.org/Archives/Back%20Issues/2013/November-December%202013/soft_skills_full.html

Lake, Robin J., and Paul T. Hill, *Performance Management in Portfolio School Districts: A Report from the Doing School Choice Right Project and the National Charter School Research Project*, Seattle, Wash.: Center on Reinventing Public Education, University of Washington Bothell, August 2009. As of October 1, 2014:
http://www.crpe.org/publications/performance-management-portfolio-school-districts

National Science Foundation, "Basic Research to Enable Agricultural Development: Additional Information (BREAD)," undated. As of October 3, 2014:
http://www.nsf.gov/funding/pgm_summ.jsp?pims_id=503403

———, "NSF Joins Forces with Intel and GE to Move the Needle in Producing U.S. Engineers and Computer Scientists," press release 13-081, May 8, 2013. As of October 3, 2014:
http://www.nsf.gov/news/news_summ.jsp?cntn_id=127902

Pellegrino, James W., and Margaret L. Hilton, *Education for Life and Work: Developing Transferable Knowledge and Skills in the 21st Century*, Washington, D.C.: National Academies Press, 2012.

Plucker, Jonathan A., personal communication with the authors, 2014.

Plucker, Jonathan A., Ronald A. Beghetto, and Gayle T. Dow, "Why Isn't Creativity More Important to Educational Psychologists? Potentials, Pitfalls, and Future Directions in Creativity Research," *Educational Psychologist*, Vol. 39, No. 2, 2004, pp. 83–96.

Robertson-Kraft, Claire, and Angela Duckworth, "True Grit: Trait-Level Perseverance and Passion for Long-Term Goals Predicts Effectiveness and Retention Among Novice Teachers," *Teachers College Record*, Vol. 116, No. 3, 2014, pp. 1–27.

Saavedra, Anna Rosefsky, and V. Darleen Opfer, "Learning 21st-Century Skills Requires 21st-Century Teaching," *Phi Delta Kappan*, Vol. 94, No. 2, October 2012, pp. 8–13.

Shoda, Yuichi, Walter Mischel, and Philip K. Peake, "Predicting Adolescent Cognitive and Self-Regulatory Competencies from Preschool Delay of Gratification: Identifying Diagnostic Conditions," *Developmental Psychology*, Vol. 26, No. 6, November 1990, pp. 978–986.

Simonton, Dean Keith, "Taking the U.S. Patent Office Criteria Seriously: A Quantitative Three-Criterion Creativity Definition and Its Implications," *Creativity Research Journal*, Vol. 24, No. 2–3, 2012, pp. 97–106.

Soland, Jim, Laura S. Hamilton, and Brian M. Stecher, *Measuring 21st Century Competencies: Guidance for Educators*, New York: Asia Society, November 2013. As of October 1, 2014:
http://bibpurl.oclc.org/web/54102

Stevens, Gregory W., "A Critical Review of the Science and Practice of Competency Modeling," *Human Resource Development Review*, Vol. 12, No. 1, March 2013, pp. 86–107.

Torrance, E. Paul, "Current Research on the Nature of Creative Talent," *Journal of Counseling Psychology*, Vol. 6, No. 4, 1959, pp. 309–316.

William and Flora Hewlett Foundation, "What Is the Hewlett Foundation's Role?" undated; referenced July 16, 2014. As of October 2, 2014:
http://www.hewlett.org/programs/education/deeper-learning/what-hewlett-foundations-role

Yeager, David S., Dave Paunesku, Gregory M. Walton, and Carol S. Dweck, *How Can We Instill Productive Mindsets at Scale? A Review of the Evidence and an Initial R&D Agenda*, white paper prepared for White House meeting on Excellence in Education: The Importance of Academic Mindsets, May 10, 2013.

Yuan, Kun, and Vi-Nhuan Le, *Estimating the Percentage of Students Who Were Tested on Cognitively Demanding Items Through the State Achievement Tests*, Santa Monica, Calif.: RAND Corporation, WR-967-WFHF, 2012. As of October 1, 2014:
http://www.rand.org/pubs/working_papers/WR967.html

———, *Measuring Deeper Learning Through Cognitively Demanding Test Items: Results from the Analysis of Six National and International Exams*, Santa Monica, Calif.: RAND Corporation, RR-483-WFHF, 2014. As of October 1, 2014:
http://www.rand.org/pubs/research_reports/RR483.html